ST PETERSBURG

HISTORY, ART AND ARCHITECTURE

Text
Kathleen Berton Murrell

Troika

St Petersburg, History, Art and Architecture

© Troika Publishers, Moscow, 1993
All rights reserved.
ISBN 5 87087 002 X

Photographs:
Ulrich Ackermann
Andrea Luppi

Design:
Gane Aleksic

Editor:
Madge Phillips

Cover picture by Andrea Luppi: Smolny Convent Cathedral

Typesetting by Avalon

Printed and bound in Slovenia by
Tiskarna Ljudska Pravica, Ljubljana

CONTENTS

ПЕТРУ ПЕРЬВОМУ
ЕКАТЕРИНА ВТОРАЯ
ЛѢТА 1782·

THE ISLAND BEGINNINGS

Peter the Great called his new city on the bleak shores of the Baltic after his patron saint and pronounced it 'Sankt Pieter Burkh', in the Dutch rendering of the name, to show his admiration for the northern maritime country which at that time was a world power rivalling Britain on the seas. St Petersburg is aptly named. Its conception and realisation would have been impossible without the drive and energy of Peter, the giant tsar intent on changing Russia. For a ruler who since childhood had been passionately fond of sailing, whose vast empire boasted no sea ports apart from the ice-bound Archangel within the Arctic circle, the significance of the outlet on the Baltic was enormous.

The gain in 1703 from Sweden of this marshy, inauspicious land with its unhealthy climate at the point where the Neva lazily divides into several streams and empties into the Gulf of Finland was for the Tsar an event of great joy. According to legend, on 16 May 1703 on Hare Island, among a few fishermen's huts, Peter demanded a halberd from the nearest soldier and dug out of the earth two long strips of sod, which he laid in the form of a cross and declared, 'Here shall be a town.' With his unflagging energy he immediately set about raising a fortress on the island, the first construction in the city.

THE NEW CAPITAL

Peter did not at first imagine the new town as his capital, but his hatred of traditional, conservative Moscow and the decisive victory over the Swedes at the Battle of Poltava in 1709, six years after the founding of the city, led him to concentrate his energies on Petersburg and to begin thinking of it as the first city. In retrospect, it was absurd and irrational to build a major city in this desolate place. The climate, although warmer than central Russia, is damp and windy; the waters channelled into canals are unclean; the river system connects only poorly to other parts of Russia; and the terrain — in Finnish *neva* means swamp — was unprepossessing. And unlike centrally placed Moscow, it was out on a limb, far from the centres of trade, at the edge of the empire.

But Peter wanted a total break with the past. He had already forced upon his unwilling countrymen new styles of dress and deportment, foreign ways, and now a new, alien capital was to be built, a purely western city, founded upon the latest European concepts of engineering, planning and construction.

Peter Paul Fortress. The first task was to secure the new fortress from attacks by the Swedes, who even in the first summer had to be driven off by the Tsar. Hare Island, so named by the Finnish fishermen, was not an ideal place to build a fort as it was low lying and in constant danger of flooding. But Peter was undaunted. He ordered his Russian soldiers to raise the level of the island by earthworks. With only primitive tools, spades and pickaxes, and no wheelbarrows, the soldiers laboured, carrying the earth in their shirts or in bags. After five months of intensive work, the foundations of the new fort were laid and it began to rise above ground.

5

3. *The Engineers' House of the Peter Paul Fortress, completed 1749, which replaced haphazard wooden storehouses and workshops, has remained largely unchanged.*

Peter supervised the operation, living nearby in a log cabin of three rooms hastily erected for his convenience by the soldiers. Even during the lifetime of the Tsar it was decided to preserve the cottage, and so it stands today within the protective brick outer walls added in the nineteenth century, furnished as it might have been in Peter's day, the oldest house in the city and a delightful museum.

The Peter Paul Fortress, which occupies the entire island, is still in the shape, designed by Peter, of an elongated hexagon. The six bastions at each corner are named after his favourite courtiers, each of whom was made responsible for the construction. First built of wood and earth in 1703, it was reconstructed of brick in 1706-18 by the Swiss-Italian architect, Domenico Trezzini (1670-1734). Later in the century, under Catherine I, the brick was faced with the granite slabs that are still in place today. Trezzini, already known for his work on the Danish royal palace in Copenhagen, arrived in Russia in 1703 and immediately became Peter's master builder in charge of the construction and fortifications in the new city.

Trezzini is Petersburg's first architect, after Peter himself, and the results of his planning shaped the growth of the city. He built the main **Peter Gate** of the fortress (1717-18), the entrance from Trinity (Revolution) Square, which bears, above the double-headed eagle, a wooden bas-relief taken from the first wooden triumphal arch into the fortress. This depicts the Fall of Simon Magus, the magician Simon being thrown down by the apostle Peter — an allegory of Peter's victory over Charles XII of Sweden. The Tsar himself appears among the spectators. Sculptures of Bellona and Minerva, goddesses of war and wisdom, stand in the niches.

4. Decorative street lamps are one of St Petersburg's most attractive features. This is a good nineteenth-century example.

5. The warrior's helmet and arrow on the street lamp are a patriotic theme that appeared after the 1812 defeat of Napoleon.

Cathedral of SS Peter and Paul. Trezzini's most significant building in the fortress is the cathedral. The existing, hastily-erected, wooden church of 1703 was demolished and the new cathedral was raised (1712-33) in the northern German/Dutch baroque style (much of the baroque ornament was lost when the cathedral was repaired under Catherine II). One of the principal monuments of Petersburg, it marks a definite watershed with native Russian church architecture. The tall drum and dome with windows (lunettes), topped by a small gold cupola over the eastern altar, are balanced on the west side by the bell tower of receding tiers surmounted by a tall, slender, gilded spire with a weather-vane in the form of an angel. This slim, sharp spire, the first such in Russian architecture, was to become the leitmotif of St Petersburg, differentiating it from Moscow and other ancient Russian towns with their voluptuous, onion-shaped cupolas, and emphasising its opposition to ancient Russian custom.

The cathedral was intended as the new burial place of the now western-oriented tsars, further signifying their move away from the traditions of Moscow. From Peter the Great onwards, all the tsars were laid to rest here, except for Peter II, who died in Moscow, and the last tsar, Nicholas II, although his remains may be interred here in the near future. The white marble tombs, offset by those of Alexander II and his wife in jasper and red granite, face the exceptionally beautiful iconostasis, carved freely in the baroque manner by Moscow artists under Ivan Zarudny, the Ukrainian sculptor and architect who had designed several buildings for Peter in Moscow. But Moscow has nothing like the flamboyance of this richly and exuberantly carved iconostasis, where the hanging bells and draperies look real and the icons take a poor second place. In the 1860s the wooden carving was replaced by an exact replica

in copper and iron. Its decidedly Catholic appearance is reinforced by the pulpit on the left, a strange item to find in an Orthodox church.

Museums. Other buildings within the fortress include the Engineers' Building (1748-9), now the excellent Museum of the Architecture of St Petersburg, and the Commandant's House (1743-6), now the Museum of the History of St Petersburg. In the nineteenth century the political trials of the Decembrists and the Petrashevsky Circle, in which Dostoevsky was implicated, were held in the latter. Clinging to the west entrance to the cathedral is the low boat house (1761) where Peter's English boat which he found at Izmailovo and on which he learned to sail was kept — it is now in the Maritime Museum. The Mint (1798-1806) stands across from the cathedral on the west side. In 1991 a seated statue of Peter the Great by Shmelev was placed outside the Engineers' Building. It is remarkable in that the Tsar is not idealised but shown as long and lean, with a disproportionately small head and nervous, spidery fingers.

The Prison. The fortress was never used for defence purposes except in its first year, when its newly built earthworks bristled with guns against the incursions of the Swedes. The construction of the fortress of Kronstadt further down the river made Peter Paul redundant and it soon took on the character by which it was to become well known. It was not only the burial place of the tsars but Russia's most notorious political prison, until eclipsed in the post-1917 period by the Lubyanka. The Trubetskoi Bastion on the south-west side of the island facing the Bolshaya Nevka was the gaol of the first political prisoner, the Tsarevich Alexis. Peter's unhappy son by his first wife was hounded into exile in Austria, lured back to Russia, imprisoned in the bastion, cruelly interrogated here by his father and beaten to death, probably with the participation of Peter himself.

6. The Mint within the Peter Paul Fortress, completed in 1806, with its round corner tower resembles a fortified structure. Altered several times since then, it is still used to make coins and strike medals.

7. Stone gateway into the Peter Paul Fortress.

8. The main Peter Gate of the fortress (1718) with the double-headed eagle and wooden relief of the apostle Peter throwing down the magician Simon.

9. Ivan Gate (1740) gives access to the fortress through a second wall added in the 1730s to strengthen the fortifications.

After the Tsarevich's death the Trubetskoi Bastion continued to serve as a prison. Its inmates in various periods included Dostoevsky, Trotsky, Gorky, the Provisional Government of Kerensky and members of the royal family. The last prisoners were the sailors who took part in the 1921 uprising on Kronstadt. A year later it ceased to be used as a prison and became a museum.

THE CITY GROWS

Unlike his contemporaries, Peter considered the new St Petersburg, at first a simple port and fortress, the most wonderful place. The original buildings, which had to be laid laboriously on piles, were hastily erected of wood. The two main problems were the frequent flooding of the low-lying, marshy terrain and the lack of easily available building materials. Stone had to be brought in with great difficulty from some distance away. The problem of labour was solved by conscripting thousands of peasants, who were uprooted from their villages and brought to the marshes to drain them and build up the banks. Their appalling living conditions, the unhealthy climate, heavy physical work and primitive tools meant deaths from diseases and accidents were perhaps as many as 30,000. On paper their terms were not unduly harsh: they were to work for a set wage (often not paid) for six months, when they would be relieved by new recruits. Many of these forced labourers stayed when their contracts expired to be taken on for private construction; they added to the growing population of the city.

The Admiralty. One of Peter's earliest decisions, taken in 1704, was to move the budding shipyards to the mainland opposite and a little

11

west of the Peter Paul Fortress. The yards were previously situated on Lake Ladoga — out of which the Neva River rises — some sixty kilometres away from the city. A rectangular structure with a wooden spire emanating from the roof, the first Admiralty was roughly in the shape of the later building which stands there today and featured a precursor of its elegant spire. Thus, from the very beginning St Petersburg boasted the two spires that still dominate its skyline — the Peter Paul Cathedral and the Admiralty. Gradually the many workers at the Admiralty began building their houses nearby, giving impetus to the movement to the mainland which was occurring spontaneously, in spite of Peter's original idea of founding the city on the islands. The foreign aspect of St Petersburg life was also evident in the workforce of the Admiralty; so many foreigners worked in the yards that it came to be known as the German Settlement.

Peter, fighting the Swedes one minute and rushing to see how his new city was developing the next, provided the essential impulse to its growth, for few were keen to live there. By sheer tenacity he overcame the tremendous building problems, the frightful floods that nearly swept the town away — there were seven serious floods in Peter's time — the fires that often engulfed the wooden buildings, the difficulty of

10. The Kunstkamera with the tower on the left, completed in 1734, was built, largely by Georg Mattarnovy, to house Peter the Great's collection of grotesque curiosities.

obtaining wood and stone. Even food procurement was a major problem, for the farming land in the surrounding marshy district was extremely poor. In addition to the labourers, stone masons, carpenters and skilled builders had to be coerced or enticed to the new city. By 1714 an edict was issued that no stone buildings were to be erected in any part of the empire except in the capital, and the unemployed masons were obliged to flock to the nascent city.

Coercion had likewise to be used to persuade the court and nobility to move to Petersburg from their more comfortable establishments in Moscow. In 1710 Peter's close relatives had moved north and in 1712 the Tsar ordered that a thousand noble families transfer their homes to the new capital. There they were obliged to construct new houses according to set plans based on family and rank. As they could no longer live as cheaply as on their Moscow country estates, many were made almost bankrupt by the new expenses of St Petersburg, where piles had to be driven into the marshy land to support the buildings. But the Tsar's will overrode all objections and, having no alternative, they came. By 1725, at the death of the Tsar, 40,000 people (including 14,500 soldiers) lived in the city. A truly tremendous achievement.

A Planned City. If the labourers and members of the court came to St Petersburg with reluctance, foreign architects were more than willing to accept the generous invitations of the Tsar to design a wholly new city in what was then an empty place. Nearly all the early architects came from other countries and the few Russian architects of the Petrine period had also received their education in western Europe. The dominant influence in the new city was that of the sober northern German/Dutch interpretation of mature baroque. Not many of these early, utilitarian buildings — some jerry-built in haste — have survived, but the basic plan of the city laid down at that time endures to this day. Domenico Trezzini made a series of set designs of private houses strictly in accordance with the various levels of society to which all were obliged to conform. The nobility were allowed two-storey houses, lesser mortals had one-storey, and labourers were relegated to timber or earthen huts.

Summer Palace. Trezzini also built the Summer Palace (1710-14) for Peter on the mainland, on the banks of the Neva. Surrounded by the Summer Gardens, laid out between 1704 and 1730, it is not a large or magnificent palace but a comfortable house, with fine rooms and big windows divided by leaded panes. When Peter needed a larger house for entertaining, he would borrow one of the more magnificent mansions of his friends, usually Prince Menshikov.

Vasilievsky Island. Trezzini, like Peter, envisaged the growth of the city on Vasilievsky Island, the large island to the west of the Peter Paul Fortress. Here, at the Strelka (point), he built the Twelve Colleges (1722-33) to house the Senate and Synod and government ministries — two-storey pavilions linked by a line of pilasters. Their high-pitched roofs were levelled in the early nineteenth century when they became part of the University of St Petersburg.

Kunstkamera. The city's second architect, a man of even greater repute than Trezzini, was Andreas Schluter (1664-1714), who had designed the Royal Palace in Berlin but had fallen into disfavour after his Mint Tower in Berlin had collapsed. However, apart from the bas-reliefs on the Summer Palace, Schluter did little lasting work and died a year after his arrival. His main contribution was to introduce other German architects to Russia. Georg Johann Mattarnovy (died 1719), who began working there in 1714, designed the building of the Kunstkamera, Peter's Cabinet of Curiosities, on Vasilievsky Island. The first building dedicated to science, it had an observatory in its central tower. The great Russian polymath, Mikhail Lomonosov, worked here from 1741 till his death. It later became the library of the Academy of Sciences and is now the Museum of Ethnography and Anthropology.

Menshikov Palace. The real governor of St Petersburg when Peter was absent was Prince Alexander Menshikov, the son of an obscure stable hand who had so caught the young Tsarevich's fancy in Moscow that he became his closest friend. Menshikov built for himself a fine palace which still stands, although in altered state. Designed in 1710 by Giovanni Fontana, it was constructed by another German builder, Gottfried Schadel (died 1752), and was the most splendid palace in the new city. After Menshikov's fall under Peter II, the palace was taken over by the First Cadet Corps and altered and extended. However, the central section has been restored as it was under Menshikov; the rooms, decorated with blue and white Dutch tiles as in his day, successfully evoke the period. It is now a museum belonging to the Hermitage.

12. The Chateau of Marly at Peterhof (Petrodvorets), completed in 1723 by Johann Braunstein for Peter the Great. Damaged by a German mine during the war, it was subsequently reconstructed.

13. A side view of Marly.

14. The Hermitage Pavilion (1721-25) at Peterhof by Johann Braunstein is surrounded by water. The upper floor served as a brilliantly-lit dining room.

15. The Grand Cascade of fountains and statues of the Great Palace at Peterhof, begun in 1714, which ends at the sea canal that flows into the Gulf of Finland.

In the last ten years of Peter's reign, with the arrival of Jean Baptist Leblond (1679-1719), a French style began to creep in and to influence the sober Dutch-style buildings. In 1716 Leblond was hired at a generous salary in Paris, where he was well known for his mansions and was much admired by Peter. He brought with him painters, sculptors and wood-carvers, and set up the Office of Construction which oversaw all designs. His great design for St Petersburg, however, proved ill-founded for he based it on Vasilievsky Island and envisaged a grid of straight streets interconnecting important squares with a large central palace from which diagonal avenues would cut through the grid. Menshikov, who was to oversee the work in Peter's absence in 1717, compromised the plan, not wishing to share his palace site. He made sure that the canals were constructed too narrow for shipping, which infuriated the Tsar. Leblond also designed **Peterhof** (Mon Plaisir) and participated in landscaping the Summer Gardens.

The only Russian architect in Petersburg in Peter's time was Mikhail Grigorevich Zemtsov (1686-1743), who was apprenticed to Trezzini and, without ever leaving the country, thoroughly trained in the European manner. Zemtsov designed one of the few buildings remaining from this period (opened in 1734 in the presence of the Empress Anna), the **church of SS Simeon and Anna** on Mokhovaya St on the mainland near the Fontanka River. Rusticated on the ground floor, it has one large cupola on an octagonal drum like old Moscow churches, a low refectory and a four-tiered bell tower with, typical for the city, a wooden spire. Closed in 1937 when all its priests were arrested, it has only recently reopened as a place of worship.

Sampson Cathedral. One of the oldest churches, originally built to celebrate the victory of the Battle of Poltava, which was fought on St Sampson's day in 1709, is the blue, green and white Sampson Cathedral on the Vyborg Side, now in an industrial district near the railway line. It gives some idea of the rapid growth of the city that the original church on this site, built by Peter in 1709, was quite a distance from the Peter Paul Fortress. The architect of the present cathedral (1728-40) is unknown, but its retrogressive style, reminiscent of ancient Russian churches, suggests that it is by a native Russian. With five ridged onion cupolas (the four subsidiary ones were added in the 1760s), tall octagonal drum and pyramid-shaped bell tower, it differs essentially from the prevailing St Petersburg style. The original wooden iconostasis survives. There is a legend that Catherine II secretly married her favourite, Count Potemkin, here in this cathedral. It is now looking splendid after restoration.

Kikin Palata. There are few great houses of the new bureaucrats of the Petrine era that have survived in Petersburg but happily the impressive red and white Kikin Palata (mansion) near the Tauride Palace still stands in open grounds, an outstanding example of Petrine baroque with its curved window designs and staircase. It is a good example, too, of how the great palace at Peterhof must have looked when originally constructed. It was begun in 1714, probably by Schluter, and owned by Alexander Kikin, one of Peter's new men, who was appointed to head the Admiralty. Unfortunately, Kikin ruined his career (and lost his life) by his friendship with the Tsarevich Alexis, Peter's son. Kikin was among those who in 1718 advised the unhappy Alexis to renounce the throne and escape abroad. Kikin and several others, including Alexis' own mother, were also arrested, and sent to Moscow, where Kikin was sentenced to die under slow torture in Red Square. His splendid house was confiscated and until 1727 used to house Peter's library and collection of rarities. When barracks were subsequently built nearby, the Kikin house became a military hospital and was heavily reconstructed. Its rebirth was due to the German bombardment in the Second World War; it was so badly damaged that the post-war restorer, Irina Benois (of the Benois family of architects and artists), was able to return it to its original Petrine form.

THE CITY MATURES

In 1712 Peter felt confident enough of the future of his dream to declare the city to be the new capital. The court were therefore obliged to move north, followed by the equally reluctant diplomatic corps. By 1713 there were some five hundred fine houses on the Petrograd Side, on Vasilievsky Island, and in settlements on the mainland radiating out from the Admiralty and along the Neva, including Peter's Summer Palace. A Winter Palace was also built for him nearer to the Admiralty on the Neva, the site of future Winter Palaces. In 1710 the Alexander Nevsky Monastery was founded to the south of the Admiralty and the road leading to it became the famous Nevsky Prospekt. Alexander Nevsky, the prince who saved Russia from the Teutonic Knights in the thirteenth century, was Peter's favourite saint and he had the saint's relics transferred to the new monastery as an indication of its importance.

The city was growing in all directions in the last decade of Peter's life, although it had become clear that the mainland was to be the preferred site; by 1716 the residences of important people were being built on the mainland between the Admiralty and the Winter Palace. Not only the Admiralty but the important Liteiny (iron foundry) Dvor was established on the mainland, one of the first industrial complexes of the new town. Further on was the *smolny* settlement, producing the tar essential for shipbuilding. Peter was involved in the 1710s in building on the Vyborg Side, Vasilievsky Island, the mainland, and his country estates of Peterhof, Ekaterinhof and Oranienbaum. All construction in the entire empire was focused on the new capital, where building materials and labour were at a premium — brick production at several million a year could barely keep pace.

Finally, in 1721 the Northern War with Sweden came to an end and Russia began to establish itself as a great European trading partner, exporter of timber, skins, grain and even iron. Petersburg was also becoming an industrial city and enterprises gradually moved northwards: in 1724 the Royal Mint was transferred from Moscow. The nobility could not escape living in St Petersburg as they were obliged from the age of fifteen to give service to the state. Peter established firm control over the Church as well. He refused to replace the Patriarch Adrian at his death in 1718, setting up instead a state-controlled Synod. The new direction was illustrated by the founding in 1725 of the Russian Academy of Sciences. Thus, at Peter's death the unlikely city had not only been conceived, created and organised by him, but was flourishing.

ERA OF EMPRESSES

In 1725 Peter the Great died at the early age of fifty-two; he fell ill after leaping into the wintry Baltic Sea and saving a boat stranded on some rocks full of distressed soldiers unable to swim. Before his death he had changed the simple system of succession to the throne by male primo-geniture to one where the ruling sovereign was responsible for choosing an heir. However, he himself, like most of the monarchs who followed him, failed to name a successor before his death and confusion prevailed over the succession in the course of the century. The new arrangement and the consequent uncertainty helped a series of remarkable women to reign in a country that had never before had a female monarch (though Peter's sister, Sophia, had ruled as regent).

COLOUR AND EXUBERANCE

Catherine I. In the event it was decided that Peter had indicated his preference for the succession of his wife, Catherine, the former Lithuanian serving girl, by a special coronation ceremony in the Moscow Kremlin in 1724 at which he himself placed the crown on her head. But the good-humoured, buxom Catherine's accession was largely the result of her popularity with the Guards regiments, creating a precedent for all the empresses in the eighteenth century. Catherine reigned for only two years before dying of fevers and chills after the Blessing of the Waters on the Neva in January. This important ceremony always attended by the tsars played havoc with their health, as they were obliged to stand for long periods of time in freezing weather — Peter's father, Alexis Mikhailovich, only in his forties, also died after attending this service on the Moscow River.

16. The 'Tokarnaya' or Peter the Great's workshop in the Summer Palace. The stove is the original one.

Peter II. During Catherine's reign, Prince Menshikov, forgiven by Peter on his deathbed for yet another case of gross embezzlement, became the power behind the throne. It was he who, after the death of Catherine, favoured the succession of Peter the Great's eleven-year-old grandson, Peter II, son of the unfortunate Alexis. But Peter II also represented the hopes of the old nobility, disenchanted and disenfranchised by Peter the Great, who now saw a chance to recover their influence and replace the upstarts thrown up by Peter's reign, particularly the former pieman, Prince Menshikov. A struggle for power ensued; Menshikov engaged the young emperor to his daughter, but then behaved so arrogantly that the boy tsar turned against him, had him arrested in 1727, and exiled him with his family, including the boy's former fiancée. Eventually, Menshikov was stripped of all his considerable property and sent to a remote village in Siberia, where both he and his daughter perished in the harsh conditions. Meanwhile, the young Peter, now under the influence of the Dolgorukys, an ancient princely family, moved to Moscow, which had become the centre of opposition to Peter the Great's reforms. He stayed so long that eventually the court and some of the ministries joined him there. The influential Dolgorukys, in their turn, had him betrothed to one of their daughters but, tragically, on his wedding day in January 1730, the young tsar, aged only fourteen, died of smallpox.

Anna. Peter II also neglected to name his successor. The Privy Council, dominated by the old noble families, chose the thirty-seven-year-old Anna, Duchess of Courland, who was the daughter of Ivan V, Peter the Great's half-brother, and thus his niece. Her husband, the Duke of Courland, had died soon after their marriage. The cunning nobles persuaded her to sign a document limiting her powers, a sort of Magna

17. The Summer Palace of Peter the Great by Domenico Trezzini, completed in 1714. Square in plan, its unpretentious appearance is enhanced by the panels between the windows and the quoins.

Carta, by which they hoped to increase their influence. However, on her arrival in Moscow, encouraged by the support of the Guards regiments and the gentry, who were not keen on oligarchic rule, Anna tore up the document and became supreme autocrat like the monarchs before her. She then turned against those families who had tried to limit her power, relying on her lover, the cruel and corrupt Baron Biron from Courland, who, never bothering to learn the language, was the real ruler of Russia during her reign (1730-40). Anna became notorious for her fondness for coarse practical jokes and huge expenditure on the court. In the confused period after her death, Biron was rapidly stripped of power and exiled to Siberia.

Elizabeth. Anna was succeeded by the eight-week-old baby, Ivan VI, her great-nephew, but his reign, under the regency of his mother, Anna Leopoldovna, lasted only a year and was distinguished by the antics of competing German favourites. The reign of the baby tsar was ended abruptly by a coup, assisted by the French Ambassador, in favour of Elizabeth, the dashing daughter of Peter the Great and Catherine I. Again the Guards regiments, hating the German rulers, played their part. In the darkness of a cold winter night they entered the Winter Palace and, with Elizabeth armed with a cuirass, arrested the German ministers, the infant Ivan VI, and his family. The popular Elizabeth was welcomed by crowds in front of the palace, and the luckless babe and his family were sent to prison. The boy grew up separated from his family in the Schlusselburg Fortress, never knowing his identity. The new regime of Elizabeth was to be French rather than German oriented.

Rastrelli. The exceptional architect of the period was the Italian, Count Bartolomeo Francesco Rastrelli (1700-71), son of a sculptor who

18. The Menshikov Palace by Giovanni Fontana and Gottfried Schadel (1710-20). It was the first grand palace in the new city built for Peter the Great's closest comrade, Alexander Menshikov.

had brought his family to Russia in 1716 and whose bust of Peter the Great still stands in the Hermitage. His son's talents were recognised during Anna's reign and she appointed him court architect; he built palaces for her in Moscow and St Petersburg which have not survived. Elizabeth was delighted by these baroque buildings, which she watched being built and, indeed, lived in one in Moscow, Annenhof, which later burnt down. The pretty, brightly coloured buildings suited her essentially fun-loving nature. On becoming empress, she confirmed Rastrelli as court architect and increased his salary to a generous 2,500 roubles a year. Elizabeth adored the grounds and small palace that her mother had given her father at Sarskoe (soon to be Tsarskoe Selo) and decided to construct a larger palace there. Rastrelli in due course was given *carte blanche* to build the new palace, which he did between 1751 and 1756, his first commission for the Empress.

Tsarskoe Selo. Rastrelli's palace, named the Catherine Palace in honour of Elizabeth's mother, is a long building of three stories, richly decorated and gilded and dramatically coloured a bright azure blue and white, interspersed with gilded and olive green details. Like Rastrelli's other surviving work, it is so profusely decorated with pilasters, curves and pediments that it is more rococo than baroque. Rastrelli's great achievement was to make use of the exuberance of baroque for the huge, long Russian buildings. The otherwise repetitive façades were made interesting by extreme modelling and use of bright colours, providing an interesting play of light and shade. Inside, there is a long enfilade of richly decorated halls, with at one end the church and at the other, the baths and the Cameron Gallery. Almost totally destroyed in the last war, the palace has been magnificently rebuilt at enormous expense. One room which has not been restored is the great Amber Room; the walls

were covered with Persian amber panels and Peter the Great's rare collection of amber was displayed there. It was stripped during the war by the German occupying forces and the contents disappeared after reaching Kaliningrad (Konigsberg), probably on the way to Germany. The amber has never been recovered, although rumours of its whereabouts abound.

Smolny Convent. The unlikely name of the startlingly beautiful group of buildings on the bank of the Neva River above the Peter Paul Fortress comes from the humble *smola* or tar-yards, established here early in St Petersburg's history to provide the pitch needed for shipbuilding. In 1748 Empress Elizabeth, who although fond of entertainments and dancing was also devoutly religious, chose the old yards on the river bank for the Resurrection New Maidens Convent (Voskresensky Novodevichy). Designed by Rastrelli in his luxuriant rococo style, it is in the form of a Greek cross. The four cupolas on the corners of the flanking outbuildings mimic the form of the cathedral's five highly decorated cupolas on tall drums packed unusually closely together. The buildings are brilliant turquoise blue and white and the cathedral can be seen from many vantage points — a fairy-tale vision.

Work on the convent took a long time and the exterior was not completed until 1764; indeed it was only in 1835, almost a century after construction began, that Stasov finally finished the interior in a severely classical style utterly at odds with the dynamic exterior and Rastrelli's intentions. The convent was to enjoy only a short period as a religious house. In 1764, just as the convent opened, part of its buildings were confiscated for the Smolny Institute, a school for daughters of the nobility based on Madame de Maintenon's seminary at St Cyr, founded by Catherine in the year of her accession. In 1797 the convent closed alto-

21. A chandelier of St Isaac's Cathedral suspended from the marble and mosaic vaulting. Designed by the French architect, Auguste de Montferrand, St Isaac's was completed in 1858.

gether and was made into a home for widows. The school remained here until 1917 when Smolny, because of its proximity to the Tauride Palace, was turned into the headquarters of the Bolshevik Party during and after the Revolution, its name becoming synonymous with their rule.

Vorontsov Palace. The energetic and resourceful Rastrelli soon began to receive commissions for private houses from high-ranking nobles eager to ape the monarch. Two of his splendid palaces on or near Nevsky Prospekt have survived to our day. One is the palace built (1749-57) on Sadovaya Street, just off Nevsky Prospekt, for Count Michael Vorontsov, Elizabeth's long-time friend, co-conspirator when she seized the throne, and subsequent chancellor. Rastrelli conceived the house as a country palace set back in the depths of the property, with a large garden full of ponds and fountains descending to the bank of the Fontanka River.

After the Count's death, the property reverted to the state. On his accession, Paul I, Grand Master of the Order of Malta, invited Giacomo

Quarenghi (1744-1817) to build the beautiful classical Roman Catholic Maltese Chapel in 1800 in the courtyard of the palace. In 1958 it was given to the prestigious Suvorov Military School, which is still housed there. The main building is of three stories with paired columns and pilasters and a freely designed entablature, giving it a sculptured façade.

Stroganov Palace. The second of Rastrelli's great private palaces was built (1752-54) for another influential courtier of Empress Elizabeth's time, Baron Sergei Stroganov. It is situated right on the main street, Nevsky Prospekt, where it intersects with the Moika River. Here there are no gardens but a huge building in the shape of an irregular square surrounding a broad courtyard. The façade on Nevsky Prospekt is the most modelled; over a rusticated basement, paired columns rise two floors to a curved, broken and recessed pediment, now painted in light grey-green and white with darker green for the elaborate sculptured details. Within, although the palace was partially rebuilt by the Russian architect, Andrei Voronikhin, in the 1790s, the grand two-storey hall

designed by Rastrelli survives. It has a painted ceiling by Guiseppi Valeriani from Venice, the most celebrated of the many artists who worked in St Petersburg during Elizabeth's reign.

The palace was inherited by Count Alexander Stroganov (1733-1811), who became President of the Academy of Arts and was related by marriage to Count Michael Vorontsov, whose fine Rastrelli palace is described above. The rich and influential Stroganov family remained in the palace until 1917. Their exceptional collection of paintings is now in the Hermitage Museum. It suffered from artillery bombardment in the war but was restored in the fifties and sixties. In 1988 it was decided to give the palace to the Russian Museum.

Winter Palace. Rastrelli's crowning achievement is the Winter Palace, the fourth such to be raised on or near the river site. The first two were built for Peter the Great in 1711 and 1721, and Rastrelli built the third for the Empress Anna in 1735. For Elizabeth he completely reconstructed his earlier building (1754-62), but the new and monumental palace was only finished just as Elizabeth, who had greatly looked forward to its completion, died. It is in the form of a closed square with a spacious courtyard in the centre, its façades facing the Neva River on the north side, the Admiralty on the west, and Palace Square on the south. Rastrelli had planned a statue of Peter the Great on horseback in the centre of the square; this was not realised in his day but the idea of a statue of Peter was later adopted by Catherine. The colours of the Winter Palace have changed over the centuries. Originally turquoise blue and white, in the early nineteenth century it was painted a dull red, and now is sea-green and white.

Within, the Jordan staircase, where the monarchs descended for the Blessing of the Waters at Epiphany in the cold January weather, is the only part of the interior by Rastrelli to have survived. Under Catherine II, the great enfilade of rooms was altered by a team of the best architects of the day — Vallin de la Mothe, Rinaldi and Velten. Further changes were later made by Quarenghi and, in the nineteenth century, Rossi and Montferrand. In December 1837 a fire broke out in the heating shaft and engulfed the building, burning for three days and reducing it to ashes — only a few walls remained standing. Its rebuilding, however, was energetically tackled and completed a year later by Easter 1839, to the delight of Tsar Nicholas I. The palace was reproduced almost exactly as before by the architects Stasov and Bryullo, with the difference that iron construction was used to reduce the danger of further fires.

With the exception of Paul, Catherine's son, in his new Michael Castle, the tsars made their home in the Winter Palace (although Nicholas II preferred Tsarskoe Selo). The Provisional Government occupied it when they took power in February 1917. The Bolshevik coup was engineered with the Winter Palace as its main goal. Defended only by cadets and the Women's Battalion, it was taken on the night of November 7 with hardly a shot fired. The heroic storming of the building as depicted in Eisenstein's film is nothing but romantic indulgence. In 1922 the palace was placed at the disposal of the Hermitage Museum (the art collection had been open to the public in the Hermitage buildings adjacent to the palace since 1852). Since then it has been used to display the works of art acquired by the rulers of Russia, particularly Catherine II. It is considered by some the grandest and greatest museum in the world.

25. The Academy of Arts built (1764-88) by Vallin de la Mothe and Kokorinov is a successful mixture of baroque elements and the new classicism of Catherine's era.

26. The Academy of Sciences (1783-89), facing the Neva River, illustrates the severely classical architectural style of Giacomo Quarenghi. Its elegance derives from the positioning of the windows, the eight Ionic columns and the pediment.

Nicholas Cathedral. One of Rastrelli's most talented pupils, Savva Chevakinsky (1713-c.1780), was the architect of the Nicholas Naval Cathedral (Nikolsky Morskoi Sobor), a late building of Elizabeth's reign. Built (1753-6) in the shape of a Greek cross on two floors with five cupolas, it is an outstanding example of Russian baroque. The exteriors are exceptionally rich, with clutches of columns and garlands of flowers surrounding the windows, all done in the striking blue and white colours. The interiors, too, are as ornately designed in white and gilt, and unlike the Rastrelli palaces have survived almost completely; the iconostasis with its rich carving is one of the best of its period. From across the canals, which almost encircle the cathedral, there is a wonderful view of the tall, slim, four-tiered bell tower. This splendid building near the Mariinsky Theatre was intended as the sailors' church; when it was built their barracks were located nearby.

The accomplishments of Elizabeth's reign were numerous. Governing through trusted advisors (some of whom plotted behind her back), spending a great deal on the court and her whims, she nevertheless always tried to rule in the spirit of her illustrious father. Her lover, Ivan Shuvalov, encouraged scholarship and the arts, and was instrumental in the founding of Moscow University. Elizabeth abolished capital punishment, a policy her successors signally failed to emulate. Her love

27. Alexander Nevsky Trinity Cathedral (1776-90) by Ivan Starov, an architect who shared Catherine's interest in classicism. In style, it is more like a Roman Catholic than an Orthodox church.

of the flamboyant, of masques and the theatre, naturally found architectural expression in her enthusiasm for the theatricality of colour and of sculpture; for her Rastrelli was the ideal builder. By the time of her death, the capital blazed with colour and rich façades. She was to be followed by her opposite in taste and temperament.

SOBRIETY AND PURPOSE

Peter III. The new emperor, Elizabeth's nephew, Peter III, moved into the south-east corner of the newly completed Winter Palace. His wife, Catherine, was in the west wing, since husband and wife were by this time estranged. Catherine had been brought to Russia in 1745 as the fifteen-year-old Princess Sophie of a minor German principality to marry Peter, whom she had never met. Her bridegroom was sickly, stupid, perhaps even mentally retarded, and sexually inadequate, and the

28. The richly endowed Marble Palace by Antonio Rinaldi was built (1768-85) for Catherine's favourite, Grigory Orlov. For long the Lenin Museum, it is now a branch of the Russian Museum. On the low plinth in the courtyard stood Lenin's armoured car.

29. The Anichkov Palace, facing the Fontanka, was built in the 1740s to 50s by Zemtsov and Dmitriev for Elizabeth's favourite, Alexei Razumovsky. It was given by Catherine in the 1770s to her favourite, Potemkin. Subsequently, it became a residence of the grand dukes, and in 1937 a Pioneer palace.

30. *Bartolommeo Rastrelli's incredible Catherine Palace at Tsarskoe Selo was built (1751-56) in the reign of Elizabeth and named after her mother, Catherine I, second wife of Peter the Great. Largely destroyed during the war, it has been brilliantly restored.*

couple after some years went their own ways. The son born to Catherine in 1754 was probably the child of her lover, Sergei Saltykov, and therefore not a Romanov at all. Be that as it may, Paul, as the heir presumptive, was removed from his mother's care by the Empress Elizabeth, who took full control of his upbringing, and Catherine rarely saw him. Meanwhile, Peter, too, had found other diversions and husband and wife lived separate lives. The Seven Years War with Prussia was just reaching its denouement, with a Russian victory imminent, when Peter came to the throne. A fervent admirer of Frederick the Great and all things German, the new emperor immediately stopped the war and invited the almost defeated Frederick to name his terms. To put it mildly, this did not make him popular with the Russian army. In fact, his only popular act, at least with the upper classes, was to abolish the law which obliged the nobility and gentry to give service to the state.

Peter's fatal mistake, however, was to underestimate his wife's inge-
nuity. He teased, threatened and humiliated Catherine, who was now
pregnant by her latest lover, the Guards officer Grigory Orlov. She man-
aged to conceal the birth from her husband by arranging, as she went
into labour, for her servant to have his house catch fire. Peter, who loved
fires, immediately ran out to watch the conflagration with his mistress,
Elizabeth Vorontsova (sister of the Catherine Vorontsova who was to
assist Catherine to take the throne). The baby was safely delivered and
spirited away, wrapped up in a beaver skin; he was named Bobrinsky
after *bobr*, beaver.

After six months of Peter's reign, Catherine, in the manner of
Elizabeth before her, with the help of Grigory Orlov and his four brothers, also Guards officers, and the elite Guards regiments themselves, led

31. The Grotto in the grounds of the Catherine Palace at Tsarskoe Selo by Rastrelli (1753-7).

32. Smolny Convent Cathedral by Rastrelli (1748-64) is in the exuberant rococo style. A convent only briefly, it was soon transformed into a school for daughters of the nobility.

a successful dawn coup and took the throne from her husband. Only eight days later, Peter, held prisoner at his estate at Ropsha, was murdered by his guards, allegedly not on Catherine's orders, although his death was very convenient for her. She could then have made herself regent of the seven-year-old prince, Paul, but declined to do so, ruling as empress for a third of a century, until her death in 1796.

Catherine the Great. The former German princess was to prove a most remarkable empress, a hard worker, methodical, sometimes cruel, with a strong intellectual streak evident in her correspondence with Voltaire and Diderot, a patron of the arts who amassed a wonderful collection of art, and a writer of moral plays and several diaries. She enjoyed an active love life and as she got older her lovers grew steadily younger, until the last was forty years her junior.

Her reign was politically eventful. For a large part of it, Russia was at war with Turkey, a major peasant uprising occurred under Pugachev in 1773-75, and the plague devastated Moscow in 1771, sparking off riots. The powerful Potemkin, her favourite for many years after he ceased to be her lover, conquered the Crimea for Russia. The Russian Empire also expanded westwards as a result of the partitions of Poland, which Catherine enthusiastically promoted, even though she had made one of her former lovers, Stanislaus Poniatovsky, king of Poland. Her domestic policies included the encouragement of private businesses and the confiscation of nearly half the property of the Church. She always claimed to rule according to the precepts of Peter I, her great predecessor, and in 1782 she asked the French sculptor, Etienne Falconet, to make for her a suitable monument to the founder of the city. The Bronze Horseman, as

33. Nikolsky Market (1788-9) is in the form of an elongated rectangle with a long arcaded gallery. The oldest market building in St Petersburg, in the nineteenth century it became a labour exchange.

34. In 1791, architect Nikolai Lvov rebuilt this house for the Russian poet, Gavril Derzhavin. It has been much altered since, not least by the addition of two more floors onto the wings.

it is known from Pushkin's poem, sits implacably on his rearing horse, which rests on a huge piece of granite brought from Finland — a fitting symbol of the harsh but beautiful city.

By the end of Catherine's life St Petersburg was a large city of 218,000 inhabitants, of whom nearly a tenth were foreigners. This does not include the many thousands of transient peasants who flowed in and out, working in summer on the building sites or in winter cutting ice. Germans made up the majority of foreigners, but by Catherine's time the British were arriving in considerable numbers and came a close second. Among the foreign builders was a Scot, Charles Cameron, who was to become Catherine's favourite architect.

Catherine determined architectural taste just as she dominated everything else around her. She continued to keep her court at St Petersburg rather than Moscow and by this time the nobility had become used to it. Although after Peter III's decree they were no longer obliged to serve at court and could therefore live away from the capital, many chose to keep a foot in each camp and maintain houses in both Petersburg and Moscow. So Petersburg had become a large imperial city organised around the court, surpassing Moscow in population, with suitable country properties not far away. Within the city of mansions, churches, and practical buildings like the Nikolsky market (1789), life was more comfortable than it had been under Peter the Great. Catherine, having established herself firmly in power, set out to embellish the capital of her empire.

Catherine's Early Buildings. Although, after ascending the throne, she continued to live in the Winter Palace and the palace at Tsarskoe Selo, two of Rastrelli's greatest creations, Catherine turned her back on flamboyant baroque. Rastrelli, no longer in fashion, decided to leave Russia. In the first fifteen years of her reign Catherine found four architects who expressed her desire to move away from the Rastrelli style towards a more restrained high baroque tempered with classicism. They were Rinaldi the Italian, Velten the German, Vallin de la Mothe from France, and the Russian Bazhenov. All except the last left enduring monuments in St Petersburg. Catherine commissioned many buildings from the extremely talented Bazhenov, but most were never built or have since been destroyed. His relations with the Empress deteriorated so much that her son Paul took him up, in opposition to his mother, and Bazhenov's best St Petersburg works (he has several mansions in Moscow) belong to the Pauline reign.

Rinaldi. Antonio Rinaldi (1710-94) was brought to Russia by Kyril Razumovsky, younger brother of the Empress Elizabeth's morganatic husband, the former choir boy Alexei Razumovsky. Rinaldi is responsible for the two-storey, modestly baroque palace at the royal estate at **Oranienbaum** built for Peter III (1758-62) and the Chinese Pavilion with its fantastic chinoiserie interiors. The Sliding Hill Pavilion with its strange tall hat design was also by him.

Marble Palace. But his most remarkable building is the Marble Palace (1768-85), built for Catherine's favourite, Count Grigory Orlov, who had helped her to the throne. In a prime position on the Neva between the Summer and Winter Palaces, this large mansion was faced with granite and delicately coloured marbles from Siberia. Marble was only discovered in Russia and exploited in the middle of the eighteenth century, so the palace was unique for its day. The whole effect is of an imposing, pastel-shaded building which faces both the Neva and Summer Gardens. Entry is through a courtyard charmingly topped by a small baroque tower and clock which offsets the severity of the façade. The interiors are rich and varied but are the work of nineteenth-century architects; only the marble staircase and part of the Marble Hall survives of the original.

Orlov remained Catherine's lover until 1773, when he was replaced by Vasilchikov. Catherine did not throw out her old lovers but kept them on in various useful capacities: Orlov continued to serve her until the end of his days (1734-83) as a field marshal of the artillery. In 1771 he successfully put down the uprising in Moscow caused by an outbreak of the plague; in remembrance of this the Orlov gates in Tsarskoe Selo were built, also by Rinaldi. At Orlov's death the Marble Palace reverted to the state and after Catherine's death was given by her son Paul to Stanislaus Poniatovsky, another former lover, whom Catherine had made king of Poland. It was then used by various grand princes, the last being Konstantin Konstantinovich, who died in 1915. In 1937 it was turned into the Lenin Museum, and since the overthrow of the Communist Party, it has become a branch of the Russian Museum.

Velten. Yury Matveevich Velten (1730-1801), son of Peter the Great's cook who had come from Danzig in 1703, was the only German architect to work for the German-born Empress. He studied abroad and on his return to Russia assisted Rastrelli on the Winter Palace and in 1760 undertook assignments to face the Neva embankments with granite and to design the elegant wrought-iron Summer Gardens gates and railings.

Alexander Institute. Early in her reign Catherine decided that the new school for daughters of the nobility situated in Rastrelli's fantastic convent buildings at Smolny should be expanded to include a school for the daughters of the lower middle classes. For this purpose she commissioned the Alexander Institute (1765-75), to the north side of the convent buildings on the banks of the Neva. Velten constructed a splendid transitional-style building, somewhere between the flamboyant baroque of Rastrelli and the restrained classicism of the last quarter of the century, which forms a semi-circular courtyard extending at the back to the river. It is now the offices of the ministry of the countryside districts around St Petersburg.

Old Hermitage and churches. Velten also designed for Catherine the large or Old Hermitage (1771-87) with its façade on the Neva, next to the Small Hermitage; in time this was to become part of the great art gallery.

Velten is responsible for some charming churches of foreign faiths in Petersburg, including the Lutheran churches of St Ann and St Catherine and the Armenian church on Nevsky Prospekt. Two have porticoes and domes and St Ann (now a cinema) has a rotunda at the eastern end and is surmounted by a drum and shallow dome.

Chesma. But Velten's most expressive building is the Chesma Church (1774-80), an experiment in pseudo-Gothic that looks like a baker's confection. It is named after the famous naval victory over the Turkish fleet at Chesma in the Aegean Sea in 1770. Velten had first constructed the Chesma Palace on the outskirts of Petersburg (it is now with-

36. St Petersburg is a city dredged from the mouth of the Neva, the overflow divided into rivers and canals, which thread their way north-east through the centre, adding great charm and variety to the Venice of the North.

in the city boundaries) as a place for Catherine to rest on her way to Tsarskoe Selo. It is in the form of an equilateral triangle, with round towers on the three corners and a round hall within the triangle. In 1831-6 it was rebuilt to house invalid veterans of the 1812 war and two unsympathetic four-storey blocks were added, flanking the original palace. The church with a quatrefoil ground-plan and vertical red and white stripes like sugar candy is finished with lanterns, Gothic pinnacles and elongated cupolas. It was wonderfully restored in the mid-sixties, although the original spire was not replaced (it was close to the front line during the siege and was damaged by shell-fire).

Vallin de la Mothe. Jean-Baptist-Michel Vallin de la Mothe (1729-1800) arrived in Russia from France in 1759 at the invitation of Count Shuvalov, the founder of Moscow University, who wanted to set up an Academy of Fine Arts in Petersburg. Vallin de la Mothe, who had worked with Blondel the Younger in Paris, remained in Russia until 1776 and is associated with the moderation of the early classical buildings of Catherine's reign, in contrast to the exuberance of Elizabeth's baroque, although his tendency to modelling reveals some of the latter's influence.

Small Hermitage. One of Vallin de la Mothe's earliest works is the Small Hermitage, begun in 1764, the second year of Catherine's reign, but not completed until eleven years later. This narrow building, next to the Winter Palace and connected to Catherine's private apartments by a passageway, was intended by the Empress as a private retreat on the model of Rastrelli's Hermitage Pavilion at Tsarskoe Selo. On the first floor it contains an enclosed hanging garden situated between it and Velten's Old Hermitage next door, built a few years later. The façade on the river is the most impressive; over a rusticated ground floor is a porti-

37. The grand entrance to the Bobrinsky Palace, built in the 1790s by Luigi Rusca. Unusually, the palace faces two canals.

44

38. Entrance from the Neva to the Winter Canal, which divides the Old Hermitage from the Hermitage Theatre.

co of six Corinthian columns supporting an attic with a sculptural group. The two-storey white Pavilion Hall in Renaissance style was designed by Andrei Shtakenshneider in the 1850s. Eventually it, too, began to be used to house the growing art collection, which is its prime function today.

Academy of Arts. With the Russian architect, Alexander Kokorinov, Vallin de la Mothe designed and executed the Academy of Arts (mostly 1764-88, but only finally completed in 1810) on the University Embankment on Vasilievsky Island, facing St Isaac's. Its long, river façade consists of a rusticated basement supporting the upper two stories, where a giant order of Tuscan columns distinguishes the extruding corners and central portico. A low dome presides over the entrance. The baroque elements are seen in the use of pilasters dividing the windows and the window designs on the first floor. It is square in plan with a

40. Nicholas (Nikolsky) Naval Cathedral by Savva Chevakinsky (1753-62) is the most thoroughly baroque of the churches in the old capital.

large circular interior courtyard and four smaller courtyards. This magnificent, serious and elegant building probably helped to confirm Catherine in her instinct for the austerity of classical architecture. The round vestibule within still retains its original decor; it has a marvellous double staircase with Ionic columns. In front of it are two Egyptian sphinxes from about 1300 BC, placed there by Konstantin Ton in 1834.

Throughout its history the Academy has maintained its original purpose — that of encouraging and training in the arts, particularly painting, architecture and sculpture. At its inception, both Kokorinov and Vallin de la Mothe taught at the Academy and Ivan Shuvalov, founder of Moscow University, was its first director. It took pupils from the age of six for nine years of study. In the second half of the nineteenth century younger artists rebelled against its rather narrow courses. This antipathy to classi-

41. The gold domes of Rastrelli's opulent church at the Catherine Palace, Tsarskoe Selo.

42. The four cupolas on high drums surround the large central dome of the Andreevsky Cathedral, built by Alexander Vist (1764-80).

cal or academic art produced in the end the spectacular avant-garde art which blossomed in Russia in the early years of the twentieth century. After the Revolution, most of the Academy's paintings were transferred to the Hermitage and in 1947 it was moved to Moscow, as Stalin preferred to have the centres of all educational institutions in the capital. The old Academy in St Petersburg is now the Repin Institute of Painting, Architecture and Sculpture. The interesting museum attached includes work by some of the most famous artists of Russia who were teachers at the Academy.

Catherine's Later Buildings. The second generation of architects favoured by Catherine fall into the later, more confidently classical phase. They include the Russian Starov, the Italian Quarenghi, and the Scot Cameron.

Starov. Ivan Yegorovich Starov (1743-1808) studied in Paris under Charles de Wailly, the architect of the Odeon, and was to bring to

51

43. *Grave of the composer, Peter Tchaikovsky, (1840-1893) in the Tikhvin Cemetery of Alexander Nevsky Monastery.*

44. *One of the statues lining the avenues in Peter the Great's Summer Gardens, laid out in 1704.*

45. *Gravestone of the writer,*
Fyodor Dostoevsky, (1821-1881)
in the Tikhvin Cemetery of
Alexander Nevsky Monastery.

46. *Another view of the Summer*
Gardens, a favourite place for St
Petersburg society to promenade
in the nineteenth century.

47. Chesma Church, like a frosted cake, was built by Yury Velten (1774-80) in honour of the naval victory against the Turks at Chesma in the Aegean Sea.

Petersburg a pure classical form and move entirely away from the influence of Rastrelli's baroque.

Trinity Cathedral. Starov was appointed by Catherine in 1776 as the architect of the Trinity Cathedral of the Alexander Nevsky Lavra, after the old cathedral, on the verge of collapse, was demolished. Lacking the verticality of earlier Petersburg churches, the cathedral has a Latin-cross plan, a central dome and two western towers. Inside, the traditional iconostasis is replaced by a semi-circular niche, gilded bronze royal doors and six pairs of columns defining the semi-circular apse. Like a Roman Catholic church, it contains oil paintings (poorly renovated in the late nineteenth century) and statues of saints by the great sculptor, Fyodor Shubin (1740-1805).

The lavra (a high-ranking monastery) was founded by Peter the Great, supposedly on the spot where Prince Alexander of Novgorod defeated the Swedes in 1240 and thus earned the title Nevsky — in fact the site of the battle was some thirty kilometres hence. In 1724 the saint's relics were brought here from Vladimir and remained in the cathedral until Soviet times, when they were moved to the Hermitage. The other buildings of the monastery were built earlier and are in the baroque style. The cemeteries attached to the monastery with their fine statuary are among the most interesting in Petersburg. Many noted figures of nineteenth-century Russia are buried there, including the composers Tchaikovsky, Rimsky-Korsakov and Mussorgsky, the writers Karamzin and Dostoevsky, and the architects Quarenghi, Voronikhin, Rossi and Starov.

Tauride Palace. Catherine's most notable lover was Grigory Potemkin, named the Prince of Tauris after his conquest of the Crimea (Tauris), the one-eyed soldier, ten years her junior, whom she is alleged to have secretly married. Their liaison lasted only three years (1774-76), but his influence continued almost until his death in 1791; he directed the government, took charge of the war against Turkey, and chose Catherine's lovers. The Empress decided to build an extravagant palace for her former lover and closest confidante, commissioning Starov to design and oversee its construction, which began in 1783. On its completion in 1789, Potemkin, jealous of the latest favourite, Platon Zubov, aged only twenty-two to Catherine's sixty-odd years, staged a spectacular party with three thousand guests to impress the Empress. She graciously attended, but left with Zubov in tow. Potemkin, disappointed, returned to the south, fell ill, and died two years later.

The palace was a milestone in the history of Catherine's taste and Russian architecture, its noble simplicity more Greek than Roman. Its features are plain: a long, yellow, two-storey building with a portico of six Tuscan columns at the entrance, and above that a low dome, flanked by extensive wings. Its smooth, flat walls, devoid of decoration except for the tall simple windows surmounted by a frieze of triglyphs and metopes, became a model for similar mansions for the Russian nobility everywhere in the empire. Its plain façade contrasted superbly with the rich interior. Beyond the entrance hall is a long, oval hall lined with white marble columns (eighteen pairs on each side), which led into a magnificent enclosed winter garden heated by hot-water pipes inside the columns. Built in a then sparsely settled part of Petersburg, the palace had large gardens reaching to the Neva — today the huge garden behind is a children's park.

On Potemkin's death Catherine took over the palace, but Paul, in a fit of hatred of his mother, subsequently carried off all the furnishings — even the tiled stoves — to his new Michael Castle, and gave the building to the Horse Guards as their barracks. The marvellous Hall of Columns was used as stables. In 1905 the palace was refurbished and altered for use as the Duma, the new parliament. The winter garden was converted into the debating chamber and the open colonnade was filled in. In February 1917, following the Tsar's abdication, the palace became the offices of the Provisional Government and the Petrograd Soviet. After the Revolution, the Duma ceased to exist and the palace was used for various Soviet congresses. Finally it became the Higher Party School. Since 1991 it has again been opened to the public and can even be rented for large meetings.

Quarenghi. Giacomo Quarenghi (1744-1817), who arrived from Italy in 1780, was one of the most gifted and most prolific architects of Catherine's reign. He had steeped himself in the architecture of antiquity in Italy and was particularly influenced by the work of Palladio. Thus he brought a mature understanding of the classical style to the architecture of Catherine's reign, which had been moving steadily in that direction. His pavilions in Tsarskoe Selo, his palaces and buildings for the Empress, and his many private commissions gave him scope to fully develop his style. The admirable English Palace he built (1781-89) at Peterhof was, sadly, destroyed in enemy action in 1942. The perfectly proportioned Alexander Palace at Tsarskoe Selo, Nicholas II's favourite home, was followed by the building of the Smolny Institute.

Smolny Institute. Designed as a purpose-built school for the daughters of the nobility, the severely classical building (1806-8) with a portico of eight columns and pediment over the rusticated ground floor contrasts sharply with Rastrelli's rococo convent next door. The great hall has Corinthian columns and a plasterwork frieze. Classrooms and dormitories were entered from long corridors. The two hundred girls aged six to eighteen wore different coloured uniforms according to their classes. They received a good education, including instructions in the natural sciences, and the best pupils would be invited to serve at court. The gatehouses in classical style were added, surprisingly, in 1923, an illustration of how Soviet architects had taken up the classicism of this period.

The building was subsequently involved in major political events: the Petrograd Soviet, led by Trotsky and dominated by the Bolsheviks, established its headquarters here, near the Tauride Palace, in the summer of 1917. It was from here that the Bolsheviks organised the coup of October 1917 that brought about the Revolution. Lenin lived and worked here until March 1918, when the government moved to Moscow. It remained the Leningrad Party Headquarters until 1991. It has now been taken over by the mayor's office of Petersburg.

State Bank. But Quarenghi's masterpiece is the State Bank (Assignatsiony), built (1783-90) between Sadovaya Street and the Griboyedov (Catherine) Canal and set in a large garden. It is most unlike later traditional banks, more a country estate. A large horseshoe-shaped building for the depositories encircles the main building at the centre, which is connected to the depositories by galleries, now built over. The central block has three storeys with portico and pediment and statues on the roof. The wrought-iron fencing, added in 1817 by Rusca, is unusually elegant. It is now the Voznesensky Economic Institute.

49. One of the Rostral Columns by Thomas de Thomon (1810) that make impressive silhouettes at the head of the Strelka. The columns, like those of ancient Rome, were decorated with the prows of ships and meant to commemorate naval victories.

50. The Beloselsky-Belozersky Palace, facing both Nevsky Prospekt and the Fontanka River, was built by Andrei Shtakenshneider (1846), imitating the Russian baroque style of the Rastrelli period a century earlier.

Hermitage Theatre. Quarenghi also designed the lovely Hermitage Theatre, one of the many 'Hermitages' attached to the Winter Palace. Catherine, who loved the theatre and even wrote a few plays herself, wanted a small theatre for the court which would have easy access to the palace. It is connected by galleries to the palace on the Neva next to the canal. A serene façade with columns above a rusticated ground floor overlooks the river, while inside the amphitheatre is richly decorated in pink artificial marble columns that ring the auditorium, with statues in niches and bas-reliefs of theatrical personalities. In 1909 Diaghilev, at the invitation of Grand Duke Vladimir Alexandrovich, used it to rehearse his ballets.

Cameron. Of all Catherine's many architects, her favourite was probably Charles Cameron (*c.*1743-1812). A Scot of Jacobite sympathies, although born and brought up in London, he was well versed, like the Adam brothers, in Roman antiquities. His drawings of Roman baths were exhibited in London. He was persuaded to come to Russia by one of Catherine's envoys and made his way to her court about 1779. His superb taste delighted the Empress — not only did he design gracious buildings in a chaste but elegant interpretation of classical architecture, but they were to a human scale, they could be lived in. His work was mostly for the royal estates just outside Petersburg.

His first job was at **Tsarskoe Selo**, where he made for the Empress a series of fine private apartments, of which the green dining room and her amazing Wedgewood and mirrored bedroom are delightful. He also designed the Agate Pavilion attached to the south-west of the palace, in which malachite and agate are cleverly set together to form a rich interior. But his best work was the great gallery which the Empress in gratitude named the Cameron Gallery after him. On the south-west of the palace

with its sweeping staircase and grand arcade filled with fine statuary, it doubles as a picture gallery with wonderful views across the park.

Catherine invited Cameron to design the palace for her son at **Pavlovsk**, which he did (1782-6), but Paul, who did not share his mother's taste, demanded that Vincenzo Brenna, his own favourite architect, work together with Cameron. In spite of the bad feeling between the architects and the later influence of many other designers in the first part of the nineteenth century, when Paul's widow held sway, the palace is a masterpiece. Cameron's Grecian and Italian Halls are magnificent and his Temple of Friendship in the park, set among trees beside a stream, is a perfect pavilion. Cameron was ignored during Paul's reign, but returned to favour when Alexander took the throne in 1801. He married a daughter of Catherine's English gardener, John Busch, and settled down in St Petersburg, dying without issue in 1812 as Napoleon's troops were entering Russia.

EMPERORS: REVOLT AND RETRENCHMENT

At the close of the eighteenth century the era of empresses came to an end with the death of Catherine and accession of Paul in 1796. St Petersburg continued to develop within the confines of the classical style, the foundations of which were so clearly laid down by Catherine, through the reigns of her grandsons, Alexander I and Nicholas I,

although at the end of Nicholas' reign the purity of classicism began to give way to a more eclectic mixture of styles. St Petersburg in this way followed the fashions of other European capitals, particularly Paris and Rome, but expressed them in a purely Russian manner in the sheer size of the buildings and ensembles, and in the use of materials: brick and painted plaster. The unexpected colours, the soft pastels, were brought to the Russian north from the gentler Italian climes. They successfully blended with the white of winter and the mellifluous light of the long summer evenings, when the sun hardly sets.

The first half of the nineteenth century saw Petersburg come of age as a renowned and influential European city with an important role to play on the world stage. The most gifted Russian architect of the end of the eighteenth century, but also the most unlucky, was Vasily Bazhenov (1738-99). Of humble origins (his father was a country priest), the talented Bazhenov benefited from the new educational institutions introduced under Peter the Great and was sent abroad in 1760 for five years to study architecture in Rome and Paris. Indeed, he would have been awarded the French Academy's *Prix de Rome* if he had not been a foreigner. However, on his return to Petersburg he suffered from the jealousy of his contemporaries, and when at last the Empress recognised his talents and employed him on her ambitious projects, few of them were ever completed. In St Petersburg his Arsenal was destroyed after the Revolution, but the Engineer's or Michael Castle, attributed to him, has survived.

Paul I and the Michael Castle. Paul was very keen to remove himself from the Winter Palace to escape his mother's baleful influence and hurried to build his own residence, named for St Michael the Archangel, whom Paul considered to be his heavenly protector. For the marble and

55. The magnificent sweep of the General Headquarters building on Palace Square belies its triangular shape.

56. The symmetry of St Petersburg is best seen from the buildings lining the embankments of the canals, linked by unique and graceful bridges.

furniture, he raided the palaces of his despised mother, including the great Tauride Palace, and materials intended for the unbuilt St Isaac's Cathedral. Built (1797-1800) to Bazhenov's plan of 1792, the castle was executed by Paul's favourite architect, the Italian Vincenzo Brenna (1745-1820), who altered the plans to give his nervous patron greater security. It is square in form, with differing façades on all four sides. The grandest is the one facing south, displaying two obelisks and a richly carved pediment. The splendid courtyard is, surprisingly, octagonal.

Not unreasonably, Paul was obsessed with fears of assassination; his mother had plotted with his eldest son, Alexander, to bar him from the succession in favour of Alexander, but she had died before the plan could be carried out. On ascending the throne, he immediately promulgated a new law of succession of the eldest male, abolishing Peter's dictum that the ruling tsar would name the heir. But almost immediately he began to have doubts about the new law and to regard his four sons with suspicion. Paul, who ruled for less than five years, was a strident militarist and capricious despot. Only forty days after he moved to the Michael Castle, what he feared most came to pass; a group of conspirators organised by Count Pahlen, the military governor of Petersburg, Count Nikita Panin and Platon Zubov, the last of Catherine's favourites, set in motion a plan to assassinate Paul with the knowledge and consent of his eldest son, Alexander. The assassins penetrated the Tsar's new castle by bribing the guards on the night of 11/12 March 1801, discovered the terrified Paul in his night-dress hiding behind a screen, and beat and strangled him to death.

Of the interior of the castle, the unusually shaped halls — oval, square, round — and the main staircase, chapel, throne room and

63

57. St Isaac's from the equestrian statue of Nicholas I. The immense cathedral took forty years to build and decorate.

58. The main chandelier and interior of the drum of St Isaac's Cathedral.

59. Looking up into the dome of St Isaac's, over 100 metres high.

60. The Yelagin Palace, built
(1818-22) for Maria
Fyodorovna, widow of Paul I.
This was architect Carlo Rossi's
first royal commission.

61. Gryphons on the Bank
Bridge, a pedestrian suspension
bridge over the Catherine Canal
(1826).

62. The imposing gateway to the
canal of the New Holland naval
island was built by Vallin de la
Mothe. The island, used to store
ship timbers, also has the old
naval prison.

63. The south side of Kazan
Cathedral by Andrei Voronikhin
(1801-11), was inspired by St
Peter's in Rome.

Raphael Gallery have survived. After Paul's death the imperial family reinhabited the Winter Palace, and in 1819 the Engineering School was established in the former royal residence, which became known as the Engineers' Castle. In 1840 it was the castle's turn to be vandalised when some of the marble cladding on the interior was taken for the New Hermitage. Damaged in the bombardment of the Second World War, it was restored over many years and now houses the Military Library.

Alexander I. The unpopular, ugly Paul was replaced by his tall, handsome son, Alexander, the 'Blessed One', who was to lead Russia into the new century with confidence, optimism and, influenced by his Swiss tutor, Frederic La Harpe, a declared intention of wide-sweeping reform. Alexander's reign (1801-25) coincided with the Napoleonic wars, in which the 'Blessed One' was to play a major role and become a leading and popular figure on the European stage. But his domestic policies were marked by growing contradictions. The reforms and constitutional amendments so passionately debated in the early part of Alexander's reign and sponsored by his advisor, Count Speransky, came to nought. From 1812 onwards, the Tsar became a fanatical mystic. Later, on the initiative of his new favourite minister, Andrei Arakcheev, the notorious military colonies, villages of soldier-serfs, were set up, in which men, women and children were subjected to extreme rigours of military discipline and punishment by flogging for minor infringements. Yet he treated with tolerance and understanding the small secret societies that sprang up among army officers in the wake of the defeat of the French and the Russian occupation of Paris, and that so plagued his successor.

But it is in his relationship with Napoleon and his leadership of Russia in the campaigns against the French that Alexander showed the

64. The Yusupov Palace on the Moika River, where Rasputin was murdered in 1916. It was built in the 1760s by Vallin de la Mothe and has luxurious nineteenth-century interiors, restored after bomb damage.

65. One of a pair of sphinxes in front of the Academy of Arts building brought to Russia from Egypt in 1832. The lotus-shaped bronze lamp was made in St Petersburg.

greatest talent. When, in 1812, the seemingly invincible Napoleon and his huge army invaded Russia, Alexander kept his head, remained in St Petersburg away from the battlefields, and allowed Napoleon to enter Moscow, in the correct belief that the distance and climate would be the Achilles' heel of the Little Corporal. He it was who insisted on pursuing the French army with such effect that at the final defeat it was Alexander at the head of his troops who in March 1814 triumphantly marched into Paris. The early part of his reign and the hopes it engendered are beautifully echoed in Tolstoy's *War and Peace* in the passage on Natasha's name day.

ALEXANDRIAN CLASSICISM

The classical Empire style of St Petersburg of this period, in which the severity of the architecture at the end of Catherine's reign is softened with the use of mouldings and capitals, also reflects the optimism and imperial splendour of the early reign of the handsome young tsar. In fact, Alexander showed a decidedly confident and sophisticated architectural taste, which is reflected in the buildings of his reign. No longer was the monarch interested only in palaces, as Catherine was, but in public buildings and even modest housing. Alexander formed an influential committee to which plans had to be submitted and approved even for the smallest houses. Thus, a consistent classical style was ensured throughout Alexander's and even most of Nicholas' reign, thereby adding immeasurably to the stability and endurance of Petersburg architecture. Classical architecture it still was but, as knowledge of the ancient world became deeper, leaning more towards Greece, rather than to Rome.

Kazan Cathedral. One of the earliest buildings of Alexander's reign was the Kazan Cathedral (1801-11). This was meant to accommodate the miraculous icon of the Virgin of Kazan, which had been brought from Moscow to Petersburg in 1710, as a mark of the new capital's permanence and dignity, and placed in the church of the Nativity of the Virgin. It was decided at the end of the eighteenth century to build a new church especially to house the icon, and Quarenghi was commissioned to execute it. But Catherine died and Quarenghi, as the chief architect of the new emperor's hated mother, was out of favour. Andrei Voronikhin (1759-1814), a serf of the Stroganovs who had been educated with the best Russian architects and then sent abroad to Paris and Rome, was picked by Paul and his close advisor, Count Alexander Stroganov, to design the cathedral.

Voronikhin used St Peter's in Rome as his inspiration, with the idea of the great colonnaded piazza, four columns deep, facing Nevsky Prospekt. The cathedral is in the form of a Latin cross parallel to Nevsky Prospekt (which runs east from the Neva) with the piazza on the north side facing the street, making it appear as if the main entrance is from the Prospekt. A similar colonnade planned for the south side was unfortunately never built. The splendid dome on the high drum was made of iron, the first metal dome in the world, but it was replaced by a copper dome after being damaged in the Second World War. The exterior is richly decorated with relief panels and sculptured figures in niches by Martos and Shubin, among others. Within, columns with Corinthian capitals support the coffered barrel vault of the rich interior. The great north doors are copies of Ghiberti's Gates of Paradise from the Baptistery in Florence. In 1813 the great Field Marshal Kutuzov was entombed there, on the spot where he made his devotions before setting out to meet the

French at Smolensk. It became home to many trophies of the 1812 war, like the 103 banners and eagles captured from the French and the keys of 25 captured western cities. In the Second World War it was the custom to swear loyalty to the country and Leningrad at Kutuzov's grave. Kazan Cathedral has now been returned to the Russian Orthodox Church and the obnoxious anti-religious museum that occupied it for so long has been closed.

The Strelka. The **Exchange** forms the compositional centre of the splendid buildings of the Strelka and faces the Neva between the two red Rostral Columns. Columns became the leitmotif of Petersburg as the Greek influence began to make itself felt. The noble building of the Exchange (1805-10), planned by Zakharov in 1804 but designed and ex-

67. The granite Alexander Column by Montferrand was erected in the centre of Palace Square in 1832 in honour of the victory over Napoleon. Only its sheer weight holds it in place.

ecuted by the French architect Thomas de Thomon, is like a temple of the classical period, modelled on the basilica at Paestum. It was positioned on the Strelka (Point) at the head of Vasilievsky Island, on the site of an earlier Exchange which had been established by Peter I. Rectangular in shape on a high foundation, it is surrounded by columns of the simple Doric order. Inside, there is one spacious hall with a coffered ceiling which since 1940 has housed the Naval Museum established by Peter the Great, one of the oldest museums in the country.

Rostral Columns. Raised in 1810 and designed by de Thomon, the Rostral Columns mimic those of Roman times which, adorned with prows of ships, were intended to celebrate naval victories. The St Petersburg columns, also used as beacons or lighthouses, are still fitted

68. The Greek-like Exchange, by Thomas de Thomon (1805-1816), forms the centre of the ensemble at the Strelka, the point of Vasilievsky Island facing the Winter Palace and the Peter Paul Fortress.

69. The main façade of the Yelagin Palace, built by Rossi ten years after the Exchange, illustrates the move away from the simplicity of the Greek to the more complex Roman forms of classical architecture.

with gas lamps that are lit on ceremonial occasions. They are reminders that until the 1880s this part of Petersburg was a thriving port. The sculptural figures at their base represent the major northern rivers.

Customs House. A more Roman view of classical architecture is illustrated in the Customs House, located behind the Exchange, with its dome on a high drum, sculptures, and Ionic portico on a rusticated ground floor. It faces the Malaya (Little) Nevka to the north and was built (1829-32) by Ivan Lukini (1784-1858). Now the famous Pushkin House for specialists in Russian literature, it also houses the Literary Museum, which means that its grand interior is accessible to the public.

The Strelka ensemble was completed by the two warehouses with their porticoes of ten columns built (1826-32) by Lukini to the 1804 plan of Zakharov. The southern warehouse, where the first industrial exhibition of 1829 was held, is now the **Zoological Museum** and the northern houses the **Dokhuchaev Museum** of Soil Science. These two subsidiary buildings stand like wings flanking the Exchange, a marvellous architectural conception in the Greek Revival style which faces the broad river, the Winter Palace and the Peter Paul Fortress.

The Admiralty. Perhaps the most important building of this era, both architecturally and because of its central position, is the Admiralty (1806-23). Because of Petersburg's development from the islands to the mainland, the shipbuilding yards, so vital to Peter the Great, were by the beginning of the nineteenth century situated in the very heart of the city. The Admiralty yards had expanded as need dictated, with bridges, moats, warehouses, and all manner of secondary buildings. The central building was completed by a slender spire, reflecting that of the Peter Paul

76

70. Bust of the writer, Nikolai Gogol, by V. Kreitan (1892), in Admiralty Gardens.

Cathedral across the river on Hare Island. The original wooden spire erected in 1711 in Peter the Great's reign was succeeded by a gilded one in 1738, at the same time as a stone building replaced the original wooden structure. Subsequently, it had become obscured by a jumble of additional buildings.

The architect, Andreyan Zakharov (1761-1811), was exceptional in that he was Russian by nationality and although he studied four years in Paris and travelled in Italy his work has a decidedly Russian cast in the large scale so adroitly handled and in the choice of brick and plaster as the materials. Zakharov's task was to keep the spire, which had become an emblem of the city, and the open plan of the yards, but at the same time to build a more solid and dignified building. This mandate was executed most successfully.

Zakharov's Admiralty is a long structure, more than a quarter of a mile in length, with short wings open towards the Neva in order to encompass the canals and docks of the shipbuilding facilities, which continued in use until the 1840s. In the 1870s the canals and docks were filled in, and at the turn of the century the space thus vacated on the Neva was occupied by new palaces and business houses, which concealed the original design of the Admiralty. Today only the colossal classical edifice remains, the central focus of Petersburg, dominating the city from afar. At the top of the spire is the sailing ship weather-vane, a symbol of the city. One of the pleasantest walks in Petersburg is in the Alexander (Gorky) Gardens, which link St Isaac's Square to Palace Square, past the long, interesting façade of this amazing building, which faces the Neva, the Winter Palace and, on the south-west side, Decembrists Square. In the centre is the great arch, surmounted by the

rectangular tower finished with columns on all four sides. Above this stands the cupola, from which the tall, gilded spire soars. Columns at ground-floor level provide relief from the long walls, as do the sharply etched windows at the entrances, on the corners and on the side wings.

Lavish use of sculpture likewise enlivens the façade. Sculpture had really come into its own by the early part of the nineteenth century. The leading sculptors of the day, including Fyodor Shchedrin (1751-1825), worked on the Admiralty, creating sculptures focused on the central pavilion. At the entrance, sea nymphs hold up a globe of the world and dolphins cavort; at roof level, twenty-eight statues depict the seasons, the winds, the goddess of shipbuilding and the muse of astronomy. The whole building symbolises and proclaims Russia as the major sea power it had become in the century since Peter founded the navy.

The three main avenues of St Petersburg radiate from the Admiralty: Nevsky Prospekt, Gorokhovaya St (Dzerzhinsky), and Prospekt Mayorov. During the war the Admiralty, its spire hidden under camouflage, was hit by some seventy bombs and suffered extensive damage, but it was repaired in the 1950s. Inside, the vestibule and conference hall retain something of their original decor.

The Roman Style. There is a convenient watershed in the architectural development of St Petersburg which coincides with the invasion of the French army under Napoleon in 1812, their subsequent defeat, and Alexander's triumphant advance through Europe. By 1814 the architects of the early years of Alexander's reign — Thomas de Thomon, Voronikhin and Zakharov — had all died. A new generation was to take over and the Greek revival to fade in favour of a more Roman, more dec-

71, 72. The work of the court architects of Nicholas I reflects the Tsar's taste in pompous architecture and the decline of the classical style. On the left, the Mariinsky Palace on St Isaac's Square by Andrei Shtakenshneider (1839-44); on the right, the Nicholas (Moskovksy) Railway Station by Konstantin Ton (1851).

orated style executed by Stasov the Russian, Rossi of Italian origin, and Montferrand, the obscure French draughtsman.

Stasov. The festival buildings erected in Moscow's Sokolniki Park in 1801 for Alexander's coronation made a favourable impression on the Tsar, and the young architect, Vasily Stasov (1769-1848), was sent abroad for six years to study in France, England and Italy. Stasov's work in Petersburg gradually came to emphasise the grandeur of the imperial authority, like his barracks for the Pavlovsky Guards on the Field of Mars.

Pavlovsky Barracks. This immensely elongated building (1811-19) in the central part of the city facing the Summer Gardens is punctuated by twelve Doric columns at the centre and sides, but the building is too long not to be monotonous. The regiment, founded by Paul I in 1796, was said to be recruited exclusively from soldiers with snub noses, so that they would resemble Paul himself. They played a gallant part in the 1812 war and were among the first to rebel against the tsarist government in February 1917.

Triumphal Gates. Stasov also built the Narva and Moscow Triumphal Gates. The first (1827-39), which commemorates the 1812 victory over the French, replaced Quarenghi's original gate of 1814. Standing on the southern highway of Petersburg, which later became the centre of a factory district, it is made of brick covered by copper sheeting, then the latest word in avant-garde materials. With heavy, fluted Corinthian columns and festooned with sculptures of a winged victory, angels bearing wreaths, and Russian knights, it contrasts with the simpler, imposing Moscow Triumphal Gate erected (1834) to commemorate

73. *The Narva Gate on the main road to Narva in Estonia, built by Vasily Stasov to commemorate the 1812 victory. Made of copper-plated iron, it was the largest iron structure in the world when completed in 1839.*

Nicholas I's victories over the Persians, Turks and Polish rebels. This is composed of a double line of six Doric columns surmounted by an entablature of military emblems and, on the roof, collections of spears, helmets and military paraphernalia, more Greek than Roman. Like the Narva Gate, it was also daring in the use of materials; it was made of iron, a novelty for its time, and when completed was the largest iron structure in the world. It was dismantled in 1936, the same year that the Triumphal Arch in Moscow, built to commemorate the 1812 war, was similarly taken down. In 1941 the precious iron blocks were used to make anti-tank fortifications to protect the southern approaches to Leningrad. In 1960 the Moscow Gate was rebuilt, the sections that had not survived being cast anew in Leningrad. It stands in the south of the city, parallel to the Narva Gate on the main Moscow road, where in the 1930s an attempt was made to transfer the centre of Petersburg.

Trinity Cathedral. Stasov's Trinity Cathedral for the Izmailovsky Regiment with its five great blue domes is a striking example of a classical Orthodox church. It is in the shape of a Greek cross, having arms of equal length, the ends of which bear porticoes of six Corinthian columns. The central and four surrounding domes on tall drums, one on each arm of the cross, complete the structure, which has an attractive frieze running under the cornice. It has been restored after suffering fire damage in the war and has recently opened again for services.

74. *Peter Klodt cast the four groups of wild horses and their tamers (1840s) which so distinguish the Anichkov Bridge on Nevsky Prospect over the Fontanka River.*

Rossi. Carlo Ivanovich Rossi (1775-1849) is the architect most closely associated with Alexander I. His buildings, perhaps more than any others, created the squares and streets of what has become typically St Petersburg. He was born in Naples, the son of an Italian ballerina, his father unknown, although there is a hint that it could have been Paul I during his European tour as grand duke. Rossi is responsible for transforming the old centre with his squares and palaces in the style of Alexandrian classicism.

Yelagin Palace. His first royal commission was for the Yelagin Palace on the island of that name, north of the Peter Paul Fortress, where a series of islands were used by the nobility to provide residences in park surroundings. When the palace raised there by Yelagin, a courtier of Catherine II, passed into the hands of Maria Fyodorovona, widow of Paul I, she had it rebuilt by Rossi (1811-22), who sited his palace on a wide terrace facing the park. A summer residence of the tsars until 1917, it has a portico of six Corinthian columns and, on the side of the Middle Nevka River, a semi-rotunda with Corinthian columns and semi-circular steps. Its luxurious interiors remained intact until the war, when a fire destroyed them; they have been only partly restored since then and the palace has fallen into a neglected state.

Rossi already served with Stasov on Alexander's Committee for Construction and Hydraulic Works, which also had the task of approving private as well as public buildings not only in Petersburg but throughout the empire. Alexander himself liked to see the projects submitted to the committee and was deeply involved in architectural decisions and town planning. The Tsar so admired the Yelagin Palace that he invited Rossi to design a new palace for his brother, Michael.

Square of the Arts. The Michael (Mikhailov) Palace (not to be confused with the castle) was the first opportunity Rossi had to design a whole square, Mikhailovsky, now the Square of the Arts. He placed the palace in the centre, facing Nevsky Prospekt, and designed the façades of most of the other buildings, including the Nobles' Club and the Maly Opera Theatre, although they were constructed by other architects.

Michael Palace. This imposing edifice has at the centre a portico, pediment and columns of the Corinthian order above a rusticated basement. At the back are extensive gardens with swirling Art Nouveau railings from 1907 and a pavilion by Rossi. In front is a smaller garden and beyond that the marvellously positioned square. Grand Duke Michael Pavlovich (1798-1849) lived in the palace with his wife, the Princess of Wurttemburg, who hosted a salon famous for its liberal debate in the conservative atmosphere of the reign of Nicholas I. By the end of the century the palace, altered to make apartments, was becoming dilapidated. In 1895 the authorities decided it should become a museum of Russian art and two years later, after Nicholas II had taken the throne, it was opened and named after his father, Alexander III. Unfortunately, the conversion of the palace to the museum meant that only the staircase and White Hall survive from the original building. Like most of Petersburg's historic buildings, it was damaged in the war and subsequently restored.

Russian Museum. The palace now houses a wonderful collection of Russian art, the equivalent in St Petersburg of Moscow's Tretyakov Gallery. The great collections of Russian art given or confiscated during the First World War and after the Revolution were shared between the Tretyakov and Russian Museum and the one complements the other, although in recent years the Russian Museum has been more adventurous in staging exhibitions of artists frowned upon in the Soviet period. It has a fine collection of icons from the twelfth to fourteenth centuries, including some by Rublev; eighteenth-century portraits and other paintings;

works by the nineteenth-century wanderers and artists of genre scenes; landscapes and portraits by artists such as Gay, Kramskoi, Shishkin and Repin; paintings by Vrubel: and works by the early-twentieth-century avant-garde, including Goncharova, Kandinsky, Tatlin and Malevich.

Palace Square. Rossi is also responsible for enclosing the south side of Palace Square behind the Winter Palace with a building totally at odds with the colourful palace, a grand and austere conception in striking contrast to the lightness and frivolity of the Rastrelli building. Incorporating some older structures, he designed for Alexander the **General Headquarters**, which separates Palace Square from Nevsky Prospekt. This rhythmically severe building (1819-29) is in the form of a triangle with a bite out of it to accommodate Nevsky Prospekt on one side and Palace Square on the other. The concave form of the building (the bite) gives a magnificent sweep culminating in the great arch which supports a splendid sculptural group, the Chariot of Victory, in honour of the 1812 victory. A second arch beyond is set at an angle to accommodate Herzen Street. The view through the arches to the palace is simply breathtaking. The west block of the General Headquarters was used before the Revolution by the General Staff, the east one by the Foreign Ministry and Ministry of Finance. After 1917 it became the headquarters for a time of the Cheka (later the KGB), and in August 1918 Moisei Uritsky, head of the Petrograd Cheka, was assassinated in the vestibule.

The centre of the Palace Square is marked by the fifty-metre-high **Alexander Column**, on top of which an angel holds a cross, a memorial of Russia's victory over Napoleon. The architect of St Isaac's, de Montferrand, was responsible for solving the engineering problems of transporting the statue and placing it on its pedestal, no mean feat. It was brought from a quarry in southern Finland and winched into position in August 1832 by some two thousand soldiers and four hundred workers. The granite column, made from a single block, is held in place entirely by its own weight. It bears the inscription: 'To Alexander the First from a Grateful Russia' put up by his brother, Nicholas I. An unsuccessful attempt to assassinate Alexander II was made in the square by a member of the People's Will in 1879.

Theatre Square. Rossi's genius for town planning was recognised by both tsars, and after Alexander's death in 1825 Nicholas approved Rossi's project to design a new state theatre and the adjacent streets and squares. Rossi's concept, which he had been considering for at least ten years before it was carried out (1828-32), is probably his best work, involving the creation of one of the most beautiful corners of St Petersburg. The theatre, named for the Emperor Alexander, was to stand at the head of Alexandrinsky (Ostrovsky) Square, linking it to Nevsky Prospekt, and a new street and square were to be built on the other side of the theatre as far as the Fontanka Canal. The wonderfully integrated scheme is truly monumental. Rossi designed not only the theatre, but the façade framing it from Nevsky Prospekt, the street of buildings leading from the back of the theatre to the Fontanka, and at the river, the curved ministry flanking the round garden of Chernyshov Square.

The little cubical pavilions in the gardens of the **Anichkov Palace** facing the theatre with their Ionic columns and roof balustrades were completed by Rossi in 1818, showing how early he was considering the scheme. They blend perfectly with the ensemble, which includes the

78. Designed by the French engineer, Gustave Eiffel, constructor of the Eiffel Tower in Paris, Trinity Bridge over the Neva was completed in 1903, in time for the bicentenary of the founding of the city.

important **Saltykov-Shchedrin Public Library** opposite, founded in 1796, to which Rossi added a façade of eighteen Ionic columns with sculptures of scientists and scholars between the columns. (The library suffered a disastrous fire in 1992.)

The yellow and white theatre, which closes the square at this end, with its gardens in front and statue of Catherine II (1873, M.O. Mikeshin), is more grandly attired, having a loggia of columns of the Corinthian order on the main façade over the rusticated ground floor, above which Apollo drives his chariot (Stepan Pimenov, 1831-2) and statues stand in niches. Pilasters decorate the rear façade, facing Rossi Street, and porticoes dominate the long sides. Gogol's *Inspector General* had its premiere in the theatre in 1836 following the personal intervention of Nicholas I.

On the other side, Theatre or Master Builder Rossi Street is equally satisfying. One is funnelled along a line of Rossi's classical buildings from the theatre to the circular Ministry of Internal Affairs (now Volodarsky Printers), which face the Fontanka and Chernyshov Bridge across a little garden. These buildings use the Doric order, in contrast to the richer Corinthian of the theatre, and are more restrained in their use of window bays and colonnades within loggias. The street is perfectly proportioned: the buildings are 22 metres wide and 22 metres high, and the length of the street is 220 metres. The Chernyshov Bridge over the Fontanka, dating from 1787, is also charming, with pavilions containing the machinery and supporting chains to allow it to open up.

Senate Square. Rossi's last great work was the construction of the Senate and Synod (1829-34), which face Falconet's wonderful statue of

79. A lamp on Trinity Bridge.

Peter the Great and the western end of the Admiralty. He had to design the buildings on the site of the old Senate so as to fit them into the existing scheme, dominated by the Admiralty. Apparently identical, the twin buildings are actually of different sizes, cleverly connected by an arch with columns and statues and long identical façades. To the right is the Senate (the larger building, after which the Square was named), and to the left, the Synod. Both are entered from the street through the archway and both are now under one authority, the Central History Archive.

82. The bridges over the wide Neva River open up between 2 and 3 a.m. to allow shipping to pass to and from the Gulf of Finland. During the White Nights, when the sun hardly sets, many people like to stay up to watch the ships go through.

NICHOLAS I

The Decembrists. One of the most significant events in Russian history took place on Senate Square in December 1825. St Isaac's was not then complete and the old building of the Senate stood on the site of the later Rossi buildings; the Admiralty brooded over the east side of the square, and Falconet's statue of Peter the Great stood in the centre. On the freezing morning of 14 December, officers and men paraded here and were expected to swear allegiance to the new tsar, Nicholas I, after Alexander had unexpectedly died of typhus while holidaying in the south. As Alexander had no male children, the next in line should have been his brother Constantine. It was not generally known, however, that Constantine had refused the crown, so it came as a shock to the population on Alexander's death that the less popular Nicholas was to inherit the throne.

Meanwhile, the secret societies of young officers and nobles which had been discussing republican themes and reform for a decade saw the situation as a heaven-sent opportunity to carry out a revolution. These

officers persuaded their men that Constantine was the rightful tsar and they began shouting '*Konstantin i Konstitutsiya*' (Constantine and a Constitution), which some soldiers apparently thought was Constantine and his wife. Some of the soldiers swore allegiance to Nicholas, but other units mutinied and marched to Senate Square, where they hoped to get the senators on their side. By noon the Decembrists, numbering over two thousand, filled the square and even attracted some civilian sympathisers. Eventually, Nicholas himself appeared and, getting no response to invitations to surrender, at five p.m. ordered the cavalry to charge the mutineers. But the horses slipped on the ice and the soldiers were not properly armed. Then he ordered the cannon to be fired. About eighty soldiers were killed and sixty wounded; the rest fled the scene. Nicholas personally interrogated the captured Decembrist leaders, who were held

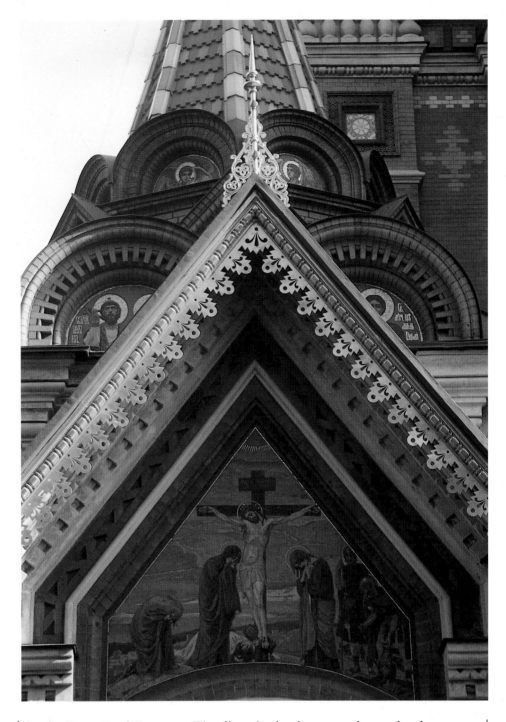

in the Peter Paul Fortress. The five ringleaders were hanged, others were sent into permanent exile in Siberia. The day after the hangings a service was held in Senate Square to purify it of the taint of rebellion. Thus, the prelude to Nicholas' reign could not have been less auspicious.

Tall, handsome, and thoroughly conservative, he ruled harshly, imposed strict censorship, harassed the greatest poet of the age, Pushkin, and founded the political police, the notorious Third Section. He ruled according to the slogan: Autocracy, Orthodoxy and Nationalism, and this came to be reflected in the style of architecture. Although Alexandrian classicism continued to hold sway in the early part of his reign, by its end it was becoming debased and a more crude 'national' style encouraged by the Tsar began to replace it.

85. The White Hall of the Polovtsov House, now the House of Architects, designed by Harald Bosse in the 1870s.

86. The White Hall of the Nechaev-Maltsev House in rococo style, decorated partly by Leonty Benois in the 1880s.

87. The Mariinsky (Kirov) Theatre, the opera and ballet theatre of St Petersburg, was built in the 1860s by Alfred Kavos, architect of the Bolshoi Theatre in Moscow.

St Isaac's Cathedral. The planning and building of St Isaac's took nearly a century to complete. The enormous building, which can hold some twenty thousand people at once, is a landmark in Petersburg; its high gold dome can be seen from many vantage points and competes with the Admiralty and Peter Paul spires. As early as 1762 it had been decided to transfer from the banks of the Neva to the centre of a new square the old wooden church of St Isaac of Dalmatia, whose feast day of 30 May was Peter I's birthday and where he and Catherine had married in 1712.

The rebuilding of this early church was never finished and a competition to design a new one was opened in 1802. It was not until after the victory over Napoleon that Auguste de Montferrand (1786-1858), a French draughtsman who may not have completed his architectural training, came to Russia after leaving the French army and submitted several designs for the cathedral. Unexpectedly, the adjudicating committee chose one of them. It seems that elements of plans submitted by other architects were also incorporated into Montferrand's mix, and slowly the grandiose building began to take shape.

Begun in 1818 and not completed until 1858, its construction straddled three reigns. The colossal columns, each weighing 114 tons, were transported with difficulty from a Finnish quarry, but Montferrand, having successfully erected the Alexander Column, had proved himself good at solving engineering problems. Little by little the huge church on a Greek-cross plan, with a high cupola and an identical pediment and portico on each of the four sides, came into being. Some of the friezes on the pediments are by Giovanni Vitali, as are the kneeling angels holding crosses at the corners of the cathedral, lit most effectively by gaslight at

88. View of the Fontanka River from Anichkov Bridge, with the Shuvalov Palace in the fore-ground.

89. The coat of arms of St Petersburg on the railings of Liteiny Bridge.

Easter. Inside, the cupola is supported by cast-iron girders, the earliest use of such supports in Russia. The interior is lavishly decorated with rich materials such as red granite, gilt bronze, coloured marbles, mosaics and paintings. Under Nicholas, who took a close interest in its progress, it became burdened with more and more heavy details, until the final result strikes one today as uncomfortably large and ill-proportioned. Montferrand just lived to see it completed.

St Isaac's became the main cathedral church of St Petersburg. During the First World War services were held inside and outside the cathedral to pray for victory for the Russian army. In 1922 the Soviet authorities confiscated 48 kilograms of gold, 2,200 of silver, and 800 precious stones to help feed the starving on the Volga. Religious services continued until 1928, when the cathedral was closed and an anti-religious museum opened in the premises. (The Foucault pendulum was hung in 1931 from the convenient dome, 93 metres high, to illustrate the earth's rotation.) In 1937 the anti-religious museum was closed and it became a museum of itself. Although camouflaged in the war, the building, especially the interior, suffered much damage from bombardment and artillery fire, but has since been carefully restored.

Tight central and royal control over planning and architectural style began to decline, and by the 1840s Alexander's committee for monitoring and approving designs all over the empire was dissolved. Property began moving into private hands and the pressure for development in the wake of the expansion of the economy led to greater diversity and laxer control. Thus, the Empire style of Alexander's reign finally gave way to the mixed style and individual expression that characterised the second half of the nineteenth century.

90. The Tolstoy apartment building by Fyodor Lidval (1910-12) has three inner tree-lined courtyards as attractive as the exterior façade with its huge archway.

Shtakenshneider. St Isaac's was an early example of this trend and the **Mariinsky Palace** facing it on the other side of the Square also reflected the change. It was designed by Andrei Shtakenshneider (1802-65), who by 1833 had been appointed Nicholas' court architect. His own house, on the fashionable Millionnaya near the Winter Palace, was the scene of lavish hospitality for the leading artists, architects and writers of the day. He drew freely upon a mixture of Renaissance and baroque and built several royal palaces. Built (1839-44) for Nicholas' eldest daughter, the Grand Duchess Maria, the Mariinsky Palace is a sombre structure, a bit pompous perhaps, which incorporates within its lavish interior the old Chernyshev Palace built in the 1760s. At the end of the nineteenth century the palace was taken over by the state and given to the Imperial State Council and Committee of Ministers. To accommodate the new offices, the winter garden was demolished and other changes made. The two-storey Rotunda Hall under the cupola has survived, however. Since 1945 it has been the offices of the Executive Committee of the Leningrad City Council and is now St Petersburg's town hall.

For Grand Duke Nicholas Nikolaevich, Shtakenshneider built the grand, three-storey **Nicholas Palace** (1853-61), which in Soviet times became the Palace of Labour. He was the architect, too, of the red, pseudo-baroque palace built for Prince K. Beloselsky-Belozersky to match the Stroganov Palace at the other end of Nevsky Prospekt. In 1884 the **Beloselsky-Belozersky Palace** became the home of Grand Duke Sergei Alexandrovich and then, before the Revolution, of the young Grand Duke Dmitry Pavlovich. In January 1916 the Anglo-Russian military hospital for some two hundred patients, under Lady Sybil Grey, was opened in the great house by kind permission of the Grand Duke, who kept some apartments on the ground floor for himself.

91. The Hotel Europe, built in 1875, has one of the best Art Nouveau interiors in the city, designed by Makkenzen and Lidval (1905, 1908-10). It was recently partially rebuilt, but most of the interiors, including the remarkable dining room, were preserved.

92. The Astoria Hotel, also by Fyodor Lidval (1911), shows his return to classicism. It was one of the finest hotels in the city, but lost some of its period charm in recent modernisation.

The Grand Duke Dmitry, a grandson of Alexander III, was one of the conspirators in the murder of the priest Grigory Rasputin in 1916. Rasputin's influence over the Empress Alexandra through his apparent ability to stop the bleeding of the Tsarevich Alexis, the heir to the throne, who was a haemophiliac, had become a scandal throughout the empire. At last a number of young noblemen took it upon themselves to remove Rasputin from the scene. After the horrible, protracted murder of Rasputin, Felix Yusupov, the chief conspirator, and the Grand Duke Dmitry found refuge in the palace. Supporters of Rasputin tried to get at them there, on the pretext of visiting patients, but Lady Sybil Grey stood her ground and refused to allow any suspicious persons into the hospital. For his part in the murder the Grand Duke, fortunately for him, was sent to Persia with the Russian troops, so avoiding the terrible fate that befell most of his relatives after the Revolution. In the Soviet period the grand palace was used as the party headquarters for the Kuibyshev district of Leningrad. Its interiors have been preserved almost intact.

Ton. The second of Nicholas' architects was Konstantin Ton (1794-1881). More than Shtakenshneider, he developed the new 'national' style Nicholas was seeking in the grand commissions he gave him, particularly the Cathedral of Christ the Redeemer in Moscow. Ton built the Nicholas (Moskovsky) railway station in St Petersburg, and its twin, also called Nicholas, at the end of the line in Moscow. To resolve arguments about the route of the railway, the Tsar personally drew a straight line on the map from Petersburg to Moscow. This was followed so faithfully that the three kinks from the ends of his fingers holding the ruler were incorporated. The two-storey **Moscow Railway Station** with the clock tower in the centre is a pleasant if uninspiring building, still in use in spite of the increase in railway traffic.

93. The Guards Economic Society is still St Petersburg's leading department store. It was built by Ernst Virrikh (1908-9), using new materials, with a ferroconcrete frame and plate-glass windows defining the floors.

REFORM AND REACTION

Nicholas I died in 1855, before the end of the disastrous Crimean War, appalled at the terrible weaknesses the war had brought to light in the Russian army and society. He was succeeded by his less militaristic son, **Alexander II**, who, although always the autocrat, was more humane than his father. His first act was to declare an amnesty for the surviving Decembrists who had been exiled to Siberia by Nicholas thirty years before.

Alexander's most momentous decree was the emancipation of the serfs in 1861; until that time they had been firmly tied to their landlords in a form of bondage. Like Lincoln in America intent on the liberation of the slaves, Alexander stubbornly and almost single-handedly pushed through this measure against the wishes of the powerful landowners. The resulting legislation did not provide a perfect solution: not only was insufficient land made available for the peasants, but they were also saddled with enormous debts to pay for the little they got. Yet the emancipation of the peasants did mean they were free to seek work elsewhere. Much needed labour then poured into the cities from the countryside, helping to fuel the remarkable growth in industrial production that occurred in the second half of the nineteenth century.

Alexander also brought in other long overdue reforms. Trial by jury and independent judges were introduced into the legal system, significantly improving the system of justice. He also obtained a notable reduction of obligatory military service from twenty-five years to six. Elected local government, too, became a reality in his reign. Although he would brook no criticism or brake on the monarch's power, he certainly deserved the title 'Tsar-Liberator'.

However, in the course of Alexander's reign small groups of radical intellectuals, disillusioned with the slow and uncertain progress of reform, created organisations whose stated aim was the assassination of the Tsar and the overthrow of the regime. After a number of abortive attempts, in 1881 the determined assassins were finally successful. As the Tsar was returning from visiting a cavalry parade-ground and turned onto the Catherine (Griboyedov) Quay, a bomb was hurled at his carriage by a member of the People's Will. Alexander was unhurt, but when he descended from his carriage to speak to the arrested terrorist, a second bomb was thrown, mortally wounding him, and he died the same day.

His more conservative son, the giant **Alexander III**, ruled thirteen years and with his former tutor, the notorious reactionary Pobedonostsev, partially undid the reforms of his father. Alexander III was in turn succeeded by his son, **Nicholas II**, who ascended the throne in 1894, just after his marriage to a German princess, Alexandra. The problems that

95. The City Peter the Great (Mechnikov) Hospital was built by Ilin, Klein and Rezenberg (1907-14), borrowing baroque forms of Peter the Great's time, based on the architecture of the Twelve Colleges.

beset Nicholas, the last of the Romanovs, were enormous: industrial unrest, the disastrous Russo-Japanese War of 1904, the outbreak of the First World War, and the misfortune of haemophilia in his only son.

ST PETERSBURG AT THE END OF THE CENTURY

Alexander II and his successors were not great builders of palaces, although a few grand residences in the over-decorated eclectic styles were constructed for some of the grand dukes, the many male relatives of the tsars who had no hope of succeeding to the throne. (Alexander III had four brothers and Nicholas II had two, all of them, together with their sons, bearing the title grand duke, and all supported by the state.) As the city expanded, the initiative for new construction passed from the imperial court to the burgeoning merchants and factory owners. Although in Moscow the intensive building programme of these *nouveaux riches* from the 1860s to 1917 transformed the city centre, in St Petersburg the great classical and baroque buildings of the eighteenth and early nineteenth centuries still succeeded in overshadowing the more numerous later buildings. St Petersburg has thus remained a predominantly classical city.

The new buildings took the form not only of schools, shops, business premises, hospitals and factories, but of housing. The population almost doubled in thirty years, from 500,000 in 1858 to 954,000 in 1890, and adequate housing became a serious problem. Itinerant peasants who came to the city temporarily to find work in winter and returned to their farms in the summer, lived in miserable conditions. For the wealthy bour-

96. The neo-classical revival received full expression in the richly colonnaded Polovtsov Dacha on Kamenny Ostrov by Ivan Fromin (1912-16).

geoisie, new blocks of comfortable apartments began to proliferate, especially in once inaccessible districts now connected to the centre by new bridges and electric trams.

Although conformity to one particular style had gone out of the window and borrowings from the Renaissance, baroque, Greek, Moorish, and neo-Russian traditions found free and individual expression, some building regulations continued to be strictly imposed. Apartment blocks could not be built higher than the Winter Palace, some twenty metres, which restricted them to six storeys. They were flush with the street, were entered through a courtyard or courtyards, and could be highly decorated on the street façade, but seldom on the courtyard side. At the turn of the century Art Nouveau was espoused by some architects, but was less dynamically expressed than in Moscow; its most pleasing buildings are found in the work of Fyodor Lidval. Architects were now so numerous they had formed themselves into a professional association; the period is therefore not, as in the past, dominated by a few names only.

Grand Homes. Palace of Grand Duke Vladimir Alexandrovich. This large palace on Palace (Dvortsovaya) Embankment facing the Neva near the Winter Palace was constructed (1867-72) by Alexander Rezanov (1817-1887) for the third of Alexander II's sons, who was president of the Academy of Arts and commander of the Guards. The palace extends right back to Millionnaya Street, where a servants' wing was built. On the Embankment side its rusticated façade and entrance porch are taken from the Renaissance, but inside, as in other grand houses of this period, a conflicting jumble of styles is found: the Moorish bedroom, rococo ballroom, Gothic dining room, neo-Russian banqueting hall, and Renaissance white-marble staircase. The suffocatingly rich palace was taken over in 1920 as the House of Scholars. Its interiors have survived intact, with even the original furniture *in situ,* more than a century after it was built. It is used for lectures, courses, meetings and concerts.

Palace of Grand Duke Alexis Alexandrovich. Another opulent palace for a second uncle of Nicholas II, Alexis Alexandrovich, was built in the 1880s by Maximilian Mesmakher (1842-1906), the then court architect. This picturesque building of various heights and differing volumes, with a round tower, occupies a prime position on the Moika River west of the Nikolsky Cathedral. Its interiors, on which pupils from the Stieglitz Art School were employed, is a mixture of styles, with rococo dominant. Alexis, a tall and heavy man, was famous for his success with women. As Admiral of the Russian Navy, was held to account for the poor showing of the Russian fleet in the 1904 Russo-Japanese War. He died in 1908 and in 1913 the city authorities debated the idea of taking the palace under its wing and opening the gardens to the public. But part of the gardens had already been purchased by a chocolate manufacturer and a year later the First World War broke out. Since 1985 part of the Institute of Russian Literature under the Academy of Sciences, the palace is undergoing much needed restoration.

Polovtsov Mansion. This pleasant two-storey house on Herzen Street belonged in the eighteenth century to Count Golovkin and then to Prince Gagarin. It was rebuilt in the 1830s by the architect A. Pel in the late classical style and acquired in the 1860s by Alexander Alexandrovich Polovtsov, a senator and chairman of the Russian Historical Society, who was the son-in-law of Baron Stieglitz, one of the richest men in St Petersburg in the mid-nineteenth century. Polovstov's diaries give a vivid picture of society life of this period. During his tenure the interiors were redesigned by Nikolai Bryullo (1826-1885) and Mesmakher in the heavy eclectic-rococo style, producing a series of richly decorated halls that exhibit an astonishing range of marble and malachite and heavy plaster-work, all finely crafted.

Museums. Stieglitz Museum. In the second half of the nineteenth century wealthy patrons of the arts and of charitable organisations outside the court began to appear in St Petersburg. Among the most generous was the shy banker and factory owner, Alexander Lyudvigovich Stieglitz. His stockbroker father, a converted Jew who came from Germany, had accumulated a huge fortune and was made a baron by Nicholas I. Stieglitz inherited from his father thirty million roubles and, although he was a student of the classics, felt obliged to enter the family banking firm. In a quarter of a century he had made so much money that he retired and was able to live well on the interest, some four million a year. It was then that his wife died, leaving him with their adopted daughter — perhaps the illegitimate child of Grand Duke Michael Pavlovich. She later married Alexander Polovtsov (see above), a highly educated young man with an extensive library, who persuaded the Baron to take an interest in the commercial arts, then a new field. In 1876 the Baron gave a million roubles towards the building of an applied art school, which opened in 1881.

The first director, the architect, Maximilian Mesmakher, then convinced the Baron that a museum of artefacts showing the best furniture, metalwork, carving, china, tapestries, paintings, etc. from all around the world would greatly assist the students in their studies. So the unique museum was conceived and built to Mesmakher's design, the lush interiors (which survive) in contrast to the severe, rusticated exterior. The

Baron, who died in 1884, never saw the completed museum, to which he donated five million roubles for its construction, a huge sum that enabled it to be financed from the income on the capital. Before the First World War it contained 30,000 items of great value and variety, including Flemish tapestries, Tiepolo paintings, glass and embroidery.

In 1918 it became a school for the decorative arts and most of the collection was later removed to the Hermitage and other museums. In 1945 it was decided to found a school of industrial art and reopen the museum, but only a small part of the collection was ever returned. Nowadays the museum is in a decrepit state, and it is hard to imagine that once orchids were grown there for the students to paint.

Suvorov Museum. The museum in St Petersburg devoted to the life of Russia's most famous soldier, Count Alexander Suvorov (1730-1800), is a fine example of the fashion at the end of the century for the romantic revival, expressed both in architecture and in nostalgia for Russian history. Among Suvorov's military exploits was his leadership in 1798 (when he was nearly seventy) of the intrepid escape of his army, surrounded by hostile French troops, over the difficult St Gotthard pass in the Swiss Alps. The architects Alexander Gogen (1856-1914) and German Grimm (1865-1942) chose old Russia for their inspiration and gave the building the form of a sixteenth-century fortress and tower. The museum was damaged in the war but rebuilt and reopened in the fifties, one of the few pre-Revolutionary history museums to survive into the Soviet period.

Religious Buildings. Church of the Saviour on the Blood. At the spot where Alexander II was blown up in 1881 and where for many years a canopy protected the blood-stained pavement, it was decided to erect a memorial church. The project dragged on, the first competition giving way to the second, for which the organisers specified that the church should be in 'pure Russian taste'. The choice was eventually made in favour of the design by Alfred Parland (1842-after 1912) of the Academy of Arts, a Russian in spite of his name. In the pseudo-Russian style and loosely based on St Basil's in Moscow, it is known as the Church of the Resurrection of Christ or the Saviour on the Blood. Its garish colours, large, textured cupolas and stylised peaks are completely incongruous in the dignified classicism of the Petersburg landscape. Because it is on the Catherine Canal, it is visible from many vantage points and the tall gold cupola has become one of the city's strangest landmarks. Its long building period (1887-1907) was due to the execution of the numerous complex mosaic panels, so fashionable at the time, that cover the church inside and out. The original canopy marking the spot of the assassination was exchanged for a more permanent structure on four jasper columns under the church's bell tower, pulled down after the Revolution. The church has been under restoration for many years.

Mosque and Buddhist Temple. On the Petrograd Side is a mosque, a surprising sight in this northern Russian city. It was built in 1910 by a trio of architects, Nikolai Vasiliev (1858-1912) assisted by Alexander Gogen and Stepan Krichinsky, based on the mausoleum of Tamerlane in Samarkand. The mosque's huge cupola and doorway are a riot of blue ceramic tiles, the unusually bright colours contrasting with the muted pastels of Petersburg. It was built for the large Muslim community that had emigrated here from the Central Asian countries as the Russian Empire expanded. A Buddhist temple was also built at this time on the outskirts of the city for the growing Buddhist community.

99. This early statue of Lenin, by sculptor Sergei Yevseev, in front of the Finland Station was unveiled 7 November 1926. It depicts Lenin as he arrived at the station from exile in April 1917, standing on an armoured car and addressing the crowd. Monuments modelled on this one were set up in towns all over the country.

Neo-Petrine Baroque. Two curious buildings erected in celebration of the 200th anniversary of the founding of the city are in the baroque style of Peter the Great's day.

Peter the Great City School, now the Nakhimov Navy School, has a most impressive situation on the Petrograd Side facing the confluence of the Bolshaya Nevka and the main Neva River. It was built (1910-1912) by Alexander Dmitriev (1878-1959) in two contrasting colours, blue and white. The artist Alexander Benois (1870-1960) of the World of Art movement designed the tower with the bust of Peter in the cartouche and the sculptural group in the pediment. A tall spire rises above the school, as in the early buildings of St Petersburg. In 1948 the Battleship Aurora, which fired the blank shots that signalled the start of the Revolution, was moored next to the school and opened as a museum.

Peter the Great Hospital. The second of these buildings in retrospective styles is the Peter the Great City Hospital, now named the Mechnikov Hospital after the great embryologist. Designed by Ilin, Klein and Rezenberg, it was built outside the city near the Piskaryov Cemetery on the Vyborg Side (1907-1914), but not completely finished until after the Revolution. The idea was to found a hospital complex far from the noisy city centre and although the architectural form chosen, based on the Twelve Colleges, was outdated, the four two-storey red and white buildings which flank the entrance in a semi-circle contained for their time the most up-to-date medical equipment and the hospital was run according to the latest medical theories. After the Revolution more buildings were added and medical institutes were grafted onto the hospital, including the first cancer institute in the country. The hospital was successfully evacuated during the siege of Leningrad.

100. The battleship 'Aurora', now a museum, fired the blank shot that signalled the storming of the Winter Palace in 1917. It is moored at the mouth of the Bolshaya Nevka, where it joins the Neva River.

Art Nouveau Houses. Art Nouveau or Style Moderne, as the Russians prefer to call it, came to St Petersburg, as it did to Moscow, in the 1890s, but with a difference. Whereas in Moscow the new merchant dynasties newly arrived from the villages, often of Old Believer stock, were eager to build for themselves something different, new and exciting, a slap in the face of the classicism associated with the declining gentry, in St Petersburg the *nouveaux riches* were of a different breed. They were financiers, dabblers in real estate, entrepreneurs of diverse interests who did not challenge the *status quo*. Their interpretation of the style was less dynamic, more muted, more linear and, in some cases, more elegant. The use of Art Nouveau was also affected by the St Petersburg practice of building in long, unbroken street frontages, which limited the possibilities of unusual design on the façade, although the few wooden houses left from this period on Kamenny Ostrov show an exciting use of volume, and one mansion on a nearby street, the Chaev House, would not have been out of place in Moscow.

Apartment Blocks. One of the most outstanding of the new generation of St Petersburg architects was Frederik Lidval (1870-1945). He built apartment houses and banks and commercial buildings in the Art Nouveau and, later, in the renewed classical style. His many buildings from the decade before and after the turn of the century dominate this period; in 1918 he emigrated to Sweden, where he lived the rest of his life. His masterpiece in Petersburg is the apartment house (1902-1904) he built on the Petrograd Side near the Peter Paul Fortress. It was an area that was to undergo rapid development featuring large, comfortable apartment blocks for the newly enriched middle classes, especially after the completion of the Troitsky Bridge in 1903 and the introduction of trams connecting it with the mainland. The young Lidval, only thirty-one

111

102. 'The Conquest of the Baltic', a sculpture at the Pribaltiiskaya Hotel.

101. The Pribaltiiskaya Hotel on Vasilievsky Island, completed in 1978 for foreign tourists, has magnificent views over the Gulf of Finland.

when he began the project, owned the building, registering it in the name of his wife. Thus, architects were not only no longer dependant on the patronage of the court, but able to take advantage of the lucrative property market.

Lidval Building. Even now, run-down and with the decoration peeling from the façade, the Lidval Building is impressive and attractive with wonderfully ingenious touches. It was designed on a site bounded by three streets, of which the main one, Kamennoostrovsky Prospekt, is part of the highway out of the city north to Vyborg. Its polygonal form embraces two courtyards, the front one open to the main street. This was most unusual for St Petersburg houses and contributes to the spacious effect of the building, giving it more access to sunlight. Its façade is replete with bays, balconies in unexpected places, quaint sculptural figures and unusual window forms. It has a rusticated ground floor and rough-cast stucco on the upper floors, enlivened by coloured tile ornamentation, scored lines and panels of cast iron. Wrought iron is used extensively: in the balconies with their spider pattern, the lanterns and railings. Inside, the stairwells and doorways still bear the original stained glass and the floors are of the ceramic tiles chosen by the architect.

Lidval himself lived and had his studio on the top floor of the left entrance. There is a movement now to form a memorial museum to him there. The building is a listed monument of architecture, but people still live there in the grand apartments long turned into communal flats. The Lidval Building was the first of a massive apartment-building boom in this district and many interesting blocks of this period line the nearby streets, some with pseudo-medieval façades, others displaying Art Nouveau motifs, all five or six storeys high and flush with the pavement.

103. Monument to the Heroic Defenders of Leningrad, erected in 1975 on the road to Moscow, replacing a wooden triumphal arch of 1945. The German advance was halted in 1941 a few kilometres beyond.

Tolstoy Building. Another unusual apartment building, also by Lidval, is that of Count M.P. Tolstoy. It was built (1910-12) on the Fontanka River, just off Nevsky Prospekt, in an important central position. Because of the rising price of land and the narrow site, it is a 'courtyard-well' type of building, with a huge arch rising three of the six floors flanked by tall stone pilasters defining the pedestrian entrances, which are finished in obelisk-like points. Most unusually for St Petersburg, the façades of the three inner courtyards are no less decorative than those on the street sides, giving, with the tree-lined inner squares, a pleasant, almost garden effect and providing greater light to the rooms facing the courtyards. Apartments varied from the large — six to eight rooms — to a few one-roomed flats.

Other interesting apartment houses include the **Salamander Insurance Company Building** on Gorokhaya Street in the centre, dating from 1909, and the **Rozenshtein Building** on the corner of Kamennoostrovsky and Bolshoi Prospekts, a splendid display of medieval Italian forms with two hexagonal towers flanking the six-storey building in colours of sandstone and dark brown. Built (1913-15) by the architect Andrei Belogrud, it had the most modern conveniences: gas cooking stoves, central heating, and even an underground garage.

The Ballerina's Mansion. One of the most interesting private houses of this period is also located near the Peter Paul Fortress. This is the Kschessinska mansion constructed (1904-06) by another Art Nouveau architect, Alexander Gogen (1856-1914). The owner of the house, Matilda Kschessinska, the pretty prima ballerina of the Imperial Ballet, had been the mistress of the future tsar, Nicholas II, in the 1890s, before he married. She remained close to the court after the affair finished, taking up with Grand Duke Andrew Vladimirovich, seven years her junior, with whom she had a child in 1903 and whom she married in 1921, after leaving Russia. She taught ballet in Paris for many years — one of her pupils was Margot Fonteyn — dying in 1971 at the age of ninety-nine. Gogen, too, was associated with the imperial court in the capacity of architect, and built and altered buildings for the royal family.

The elegant Kschessinska house, Gogen's best building, has an interesting façade looking onto two streets, with a tower, conservatory for the winter garden, charming corner pavilion, and differing roof levels in a strictly rectilinear style. Its inflexible façade of straight lines is belied by the rich interior demanded by Kschessinska, a leading society hostess, who preferred to entertain in the lush period ambience of the royal palaces of twenty years earlier.

This unusual building played a significant role in the history of the city. In February 1917 it was expropriated by a group of revolutionary workers in Kschessinska's absence, and on 11 March the Bolsheviks moved in. Kschessinska complained that the wild mob sacked the house from top to bottom, wrecking even the grand piano.

It was to this house that Lenin came on 3 April 1917 from the Finland Station, on his return from Switzerland through Germany in the famous sealed train; he spoke to crowds gathered here from the balcony on the west side. From the end of the thirties to 1957 it was the Kirov Museum and then became the Museum of the Great October Socialist Revolution with the Kschessinska house linked to the neighbouring Brandt mansion (R.F.Meltser) by a two-storey addition which became the entrance. Since the end of the Soviet regime, it has become a historical waxworks museum and exhibition centre, including a fascinating display on the life of Kschessinska.

Wood and Stone. On Kamenny Ostov (Stone Island) and surrounding islands parks provide breathing spaces for the crowded city. Since the inception of St Petersburg they had been used for royal and aristocratic palaces and only in the late nineteenth century were they made available to the public. In 1895 new building was permitted there and a group of interesting Art Nouveau wooden houses or dachas appeared. After the Revolution, the island was renamed 'Trudyashchiikhsya' (Of the Workers) and the dachas were confiscated and turned into holiday homes for the workers. Later, the splendid houses were used by powerful Soviet organisations and the security services again closed the park to ordinary people.

One of the most interesting of the dachas is the 1904 house of the architect Robert Meltser (1806-1929). Made of stone and brick on the ground floor, it zooms upwards and outwards with wooden logs ending in an extremely steeply pitched roof and tall chimney. Its chief features are the height, sharp gables, mixture of materials and the sunburst over the entrance. The original simple wooden furniture based on traditional Russian designs has not survived.

Almost opposite is another such dacha by the same architect, the Vollenweider House (1904) with even taller roofs. Now the Danish Consulate and painted dark grey, it was originally white and known as the Sugar Loaf because of the unusual shape of the roof.

COMMERCE AND THE EVOLUTION OF STYLE

The modern style, often tempered with classical elements, was not only found in housing but also in the many new and expanding businesses — especially the banks — a result of the rapidly increasing population and the growth of St Petersburg as a financial and industrial centre. Nevsky Prospekt, traditionally the habitat of the gentry, gradually became more democratic.

Yeliseyev Emporium. Shops arose, like the ostentatious emporium of the Yeliseyev brothers on Nevsky Prospekt (1902-4) by Gavril Baranovsky (1860-1923), with its huge two-storey stained-glass window, ponderous bronze statues and towers on the corners, and combination of wood, metal, marble and glass in the interior. On the first floor the grocers, who loved drama, opened a small theatre that still functions. Yeliseyev's wonderful choice of groceries was sharply reduced in Soviet times, although it is still a food shop, its unchanged interior decor irresistibly reminiscent of Harrod's food halls.

Singer Sewing Machine Building. Nothing conveys the changes in Russian society of this time more than the activities of the American-based Singer Sewing Machine Company. Its arrival in the 1870s resulted in a domestic revolution; by the turn of the century sewing machines had become commonplace in Russian homes; some from those times are still in use. In a prime position on Nevsky Prospekt at the Catherine Canal, the company constructed (1902-4) a large and impressive building, engaging as its architect Pavel Syuzor (1844-1919), an experienced St Petersburg builder. The Singer Building is the tallest commercial building in the city — seven floors — its glass cupola just managing to exceed the height regulations. It is built on a ferroconcrete and brick frame with iron columns on the first floor; its plate glass windows rise from floor to ceiling, providing good illumination.

Guards Economic Society. Just off Nevsky Prospekt on Bolshaya Konyushennaya Street (Zhelyabova) is the leading department store of pre-Revolutionary Petersburg. Originally a military store, like the Army and Navy in London, it was built as the Trading House of the Guards Economic Society by Ernst Virrikh and others (1908-9). The shop is a form of highly rationalised Art Nouveau based on a frame of ferroconcrete, the first three floors using plate glass within concrete piers and iron horizontal supports. Within is a great hall rising the height of the building, surrounded by three floors of galleries and roofed over with glass in an iron frame. Like the Church on the Blood, it sits on a concrete slab instead of the traditional piles, a better material to combat the frequent floods.

Hotel Europe. Standing at the entrance to Rossi's Square of Arts and just off Nevsky Prospekt, the hotel has one of the best sites in Petersburg. Built in 1875, it was redecorated first by Karl Makkenzen (1905) and then by Lidval (1908-10) and had one of the best Art Nouveau interiors in the city. The dining room, in particular, is superb, with its alcove and central hall, wooden balcony and great stained-glass window of Helios in his chariot to the drawing of Benois.

Mertens. The most monumental of the new trading houses was Mertens, on Nevsky Prospekt (1919-21), designed by Marian Lyalevich (1876-1944). The façade of this shop is cut by three huge glass arches rising almost the height of the building with sculptured panels above the

117

106. Palace Square with the Alexander Column in the centre perfectly sets off the buildings that surround it.

arches. It is a superb example of the new style of architecture arising out of a classical base of pilasters and Corinthian capitals. Mertens was a well-established firm of fur manufacturers and the building was intended for its shop, offices and working premises. Nowadays it is not only the House of Models, a congenial successor to Mertens but, less appropriately, a fish shop.

New Arcade. The arcade or passage on Liteiny Prospekt is one of the best examples of commercial modern architecture. Here there are no compromises with classical forms. It was built (1912-13) by Nikolai Vasiliev on one of the Sheremetiev estates (a gate and grotto were demolished). A huge arched entrance breaks up the line of solid glass bays punctuated only by square ferroconcrete piers clad in granite. It is this building and the one following that lead most naturally into the fashion for the undecorated Constructivist design that was to hold sway in the first years of the revolution.

German Embassy. The building designed by the German architect, Peter Behrens, for the German Embassy is also uncompromisingly modern, with its austere and simple red granite columns rising three floors and rhythmically placed windows with no ornamentation. Mies van der Rohe as a young budding architect worked on the building with Behrens. A modern building opposite the indulgent St Isaac's, it is now used by the state tourist organisation.

The Classical Revival. Frederic Lidval eventually forsook Art Nouveau and turned back to classical forms. Neo-classical architecture had never really been excised in St Petersburg and, after the reimposition of authoritarian control following the unrest of 1905 and the rejection of

107. The Winter Palace, facing the broad Neva, looks vulnerable to the vagaries of the river. It now houses the Hermitage Museum, one of the greatest art museums in the world.

demands for political reform, the more imperial fashion in architecture returned with a vengeance.

Azov-Don Bank. This is particularly true of Lidval's Azov-Don Bank (1907-13) on Herzen St (now the International Telegraph Station). Petersburg had experienced a boom in the opening of new banks after 1900 (by 1914 there were fifty banks) and many new buildings were constructed to accommodate them. Their design of necessity had to give a grave, confident impression to their clients. Lidval's task was to combine two neighbouring sites into one, which he did with a common front of grey granite. The austere façade with Ionic columns and pediment is somewhat relieved by the ground floor bas-reliefs by Vasily Kuznetsov (1882-1923) and other sculpture. Within, this classical approach makes way for the linear Art Nouveau of the large utilitarian hall of ferroconcrete construction.

Polovtsov Dacha. Where the1880s Polovtsov house in Petersburg epitomises the eclectic style, the dacha or country house built by the same family on Kamenny Ostrov in 1910 marks the summit of the neo-classical revival. After Senator Alexander Alexandrovich Polovtsov died in 1909, his family appointed the young, talented Ivan Fomin to build this extraordinary mansion (1912-16). It is a grand house based on Palladian principles in the form of a U with a centrally placed main entrance of paired ionic columns with pediment above and circular niche. The wings flow outwards in a long colonnade with a simple, well-delineated entablature. Within, it is luxuriously decorated, especially the Gobelin hall of tapestries and the hall of white columns, its ceiling taken from the first Baron Stieglitz's early-nineteenth-century house on this site. It seems almost too monumental to be a comfortable house for dacha living.

108. The Jordan Staircase of the Winter Palace is the only part of the original, Rastrelli interior to have survived. it was this staircase that the tsars descended for the ceremony of Blessing the Waters at Epiphany. The cold January weather proved the undoing of many of them.

109. The Malachite Hall in the Winter Palace (1838-9).

110. A corner of the Hermitage with Titian's 'Danae' in the foreground.

Abamelek-Lazarev House. Situated between the Millionnaya near Palace Square, and the Moika, this early-eighteenth-century house was purchased by Prince S.S. Abamelek-Lazarev, of Armenian descent, who had it significantly altered (1909) by Yevgraf Vorotilov (1837-1910). The façade on the Moika was made to resemble the Armenian church on Nevsky Prospekt. In 1911 the Prince acquired its neighbour, No. 24, and had Ivan Fomin rebuild the section on the Moika (1913-15) as a delightful classical house of the Empire period with Corinthian pilasters rising three floors (the third-floor windows are barely visible), medallions of dancers in between the pilasters and vases on top of the attic. The rooms within, using natural and artificial marble, are grand and richly decorated, especially the theatre and white dining room. This house and the Polovtsov dacha were the last of the luxurious grand houses built in St Petersburg before the deluge of the Bolsheviks and their predilection for sparse, functional, geometrical architecture. Fomin was to express his talents as the initiator of 'proletarian classicism', an austere interpretation of classical architecture.

ON THE EVE OF REVOLUTION

The order imposed on the city by the town-planning strategies of Alexander I and Nicholas I gave way by the end of the nineteenth century to near chaos as over one and a half million peasants, freed from the ties that bound them to their landlords and hungry for work, poured into St Petersburg between 1870 and 1914 , making it the fifth largest city in Europe. The newly established industries were glad to employ them, but gave them little in the way of housing and other benefits, and the city council was overwhelmed by problems of poor water and sanitation. It

123

111. The Armorial Hall, designed by Vasily Stasov in 1839, after the disastrous fire two years previously.

112, 113. The White Hall of the Winter Palace, rebuilt after the 1837 fire.

was always a notoriously unhealthy city, situated as it was in the midst of a swamp, but now crime became rife and alcoholism a particular problem. Added to this, many of the functions normally handled by municipal authorities, like policing, came directly under the authority of the Tsar. Factories sprang up everywhere and little control was exercised over their location and conditions.

Harbour Workers' Village. One courageous attempt at alleviating the situation was the Harbour Workers' Village project on Vasilievsky Island, built (1904-8) by Nikolai Dmitriev (1856-1919), an architect and member of the Society for the Construction and Improvement of Housing for the Needy Population. These five handsome five-storey blocks of alternating brick and stucco were intended to provide cheap housing for the poor, with shop, club and school as part of the amenities. The subsidised rents were as low as R. 4.30 for a room and R. 7.40 for an apartment, or about one third of the average worker's wages. Even so, these rents were still too high for most workers to afford and only about two dozen workers' families were able to take advantage of the fine flats. Dmitriev's handsome blocks are still used as housing.

The housing problems of the tsarist period were never properly tackled and remained as a legacy for the new Soviet era. In 1913, amid much pomp and circumstance, Nicholas II and Alexandra celebrated three hundred years of the Romanov dynasty. Churches were built in honour of the occasion and the Tsar paraded in glory throughout the empire. Only four years later, following a series of defeats in the disastrous war with Germany, and growing public unrest caused by food shortages and disgust over the scandals involving Rasputin and the court, the dynasty was overthrown and a new dictatorship came to rule Russia.

THE LENINGRAD ERA

St Petersburg greeted the outbreak of the First World War with patriotic enthusiasm and the city was renamed the more Russian-sounding Petrograd (Peter's city) soon after. But after two years, war-weariness, the series of defeats suffered by the Russian army, and disgust at the incompetence of the government and corruption of the court, served as the catalyst for the events of 1917. In February public order broke down, there were bread riots and shootings in Petrograd, and Nicholas II was advised to abdicate. This he did in favour of his brother, Michael, but the latter refused the crown and the three-hundred-year-old dynasty of the Romanovs came abruptly to an end.

OCTOBER REVOLUTION

The hundreds of victims of the violence in the February Revolution were laid to rest on the Field of Mars near the Summer Gardens where, immediately after the Revolution, the first Soviet monument, by Lev Rudnev (1885-1956), was unveiled in honour of the fallen. Meanwhile, Kerensky headed the disparate Provisional Government and, fatally, continued the war against Germany. At first the Duma and the rival Bolshevik Soviet of Worker's Deputies operated in parallel from different rooms in the Tauride Palace, but following an abortive attempt at a coup in July, the Bolsheviks were on the wane and Lenin had gone again into hiding.

114. Peterhof: the Lower Park looking towards the Chateau of Marly from the Golden Hill Cascade.

115. The front of the Great Palace at Peterhof from the Neptune Fountain.

116. A sculpture in the Russian Museum, formerly the Michael (Mikhailov) Palace.

117-119. Interiors of the Great Palace at Peterhof, which was completely restored after wartime damage, even to the tiled stoves.

However, General Kornilov's ill-advised advance on the capital revived fears of counter-revolution and played into the hands of the Bolsheviks, who regained the ascendancy and in October (old style) were ready to stage their coup. They seized key points in the city on 7 November (new style) and then, after a blank shot was fired by the Battleship Aurora as a signal, moved in to take the Winter Palace, where the Provisional Government was sitting. This was done with unexpected ease and Lenin, after years of fruitless plotting in exile, found himself at the head of the defeated and disintegrating Russian Empire.

Civil war broke out, but the Germans advancing on the city were a more immediate menace, and to preserve their power the Bolsheviks concluded the crippling Treaty of Brest-Litovsk in March 1918, at the price of huge territorial losses. The new government decided to move to the safer environs of Moscow. Because of the privations of the first years of Soviet rule — hunger, lack of fuel, emigration, the civil war — and the move of the government to Moscow, the population rapidly fell. By 1920 it was down to 722,000 from over two million in 1915, but by 1926 had crept back up to 1.6 million and by 1939 was over three million. The population is now five million.

Once stability was at last achieved and the Bolsheviks felt secure, Lenin, in an attempt to restore an economy ravaged by civil strife and 'war communism', introduced the New Economic Policy, which allowed a certain amount of private enterprise within state control of the 'commanding heights'. During the twenties, correspondingly limited freedom of expression was allowed in the arts, which enjoyed a brief period of dynamic creativity before Stalin began to impose full state ideological control. By then Lenin had died and Peter's city now bore his name.

120, 121. Eighteenth-century art in the Russian Museum, illustrating the abrupt change in Russian art from iconographic to European that occurred in that century.

THE AVANT-GARDE

Initially there was enthusiasm among many of the architects of the older generation for what they perceived as the opportunity to create buildings that would benefit the population as a whole in the new worker-oriented state. It was clear that for reasons of economy and in order to distance themselves from the decorative architecture of the tsarist period a plainer, more clean-cut, functional design was necessary for the different kinds of buildings demanded by the new state. This style is sometimes known as avant-garde or, more loosely, Constructivist; its salient features are geometrical forms, lack of decoration, and functionalism inside and out. It did not arise entirely spontaneously but was derived from the new building materials developed before the Revolution, especially ferroconcrete and glass, and the stylised forms of classicism that had again begun to pervade St Petersburg's architecture, particularly in commercial buildings before 1917. Some of the new buildings, which for effect depended entirely on their form, were truly beautiful.

Garden Cities. The first schemes designed to improve the appallingly low standards of workers' housing featured the idea of cottages or 'garden cities'. In the south-east Nevsky district, several streets of two-storey houses surrounded by gardens, the Palevsky Plot, were built (1926-7) by A. Zazerkin and N. Rybin. Today, although still some distance from the centre, it has become desirable housing. Communal apartment blocks were also built in the middle and late twenties as experiments in social living and to free women from household chores. One such block in Leningrad was built by a collective of young engineers,

122. Pavlovsk Palace: the Knights' Gallery built by Paul I to receive the Knights of the Order of Malta who fled to Russia when Napoleon seized the island.

123. Classical statuary adorned many palaces of imperial Russia, echoing the grandeur of Rome.

among whom was the poet, Olga Bergolts. There were no kitchens in the flats, only one large common cooking and eating room, and common rooms for children and recreation. Within two years the inhabitants had found this idealists' scheme to be less than ideal. With no room for privacy, people became tired and irritable. Eventually, these communal houses became hostels, usually for students.

Narva Square Development. Narva Square with its splendid triumphal gate is on the west side of St Petersburg, not far from the docks and near a large number of factories, including the famous Putilov iron works, one of the biggest in Russia. Here, on 9 January 1905, the striking Putilov workers persuaded others to join them and a group led by the socialist priest, Father Gapon began making their way to Palace Square, intending to present a petition to the Tsar. At the Narva Gate they were fired upon by tsarist troops. At least forty died. This day became known as Bloody Sunday and is reckoned as the start of the 1905 Revolution. It is thus not surprising that this working class district received so much attention from the new government. Ivan Fomin included it in his 1919 replanning of Petrograd and later formulated a more comprehensive plan for the area. Two large squares with the Narva Gate at their head were to be linked by a broad avenue, renamed Stachek (Strike) Prospekt, lined with important new buildings. The first was to be the Palace of Culture.

Gorky Palace of Culture. The Bolsheviks devoted much time and expense on constructing special clubs for workers in the districts where they lived. The idea was to give them some of the advantages enjoyed in the past by the more cultured bourgeoisie. One of the most impressive of these clubs is the Gorky Palace of Culture on Stachek Square, completed in 1927 in honour of the first decade of communism by architects

124. The Catherine Palace at Tsarskoe Selo built by Rastrelli (1751-56) in the reign of Elizabeth and named for her mother, Empress Catherine I.

125. Vase at the royal estate at Pavlovsk. Much of the valuable furnishings were chosen by Maria Fyodorovna, wife of Paul I, who was the real mistress of Pavlovsk, since Paul preferred Gatchina.

126. The caryatids at Tsarskoe Selo that break up the long, monotonous façade show Rastrelli's predominantly sculptural view of architecture.

Alexander Gegello (1891-1965) and David Krichevsky (1892-1942). It is in the shape of a fan with a curved façade built almost entirely of glass, within two towers which enclose the theatre of nearly 1,900 seats. One of the first examples of Constructivist architecture in the country, it served as a prototype of the workers' palaces.

Shop-Factory-Kitchen. Opposite it is the Kirov department store and factory-kitchen, built at the same time and perhaps the best of Leningrad's new Constructivist buildings. Large department stores had begun to appear before the Revolution, but not in the workers' districts. The factory-kitchen for the preparation of food on a mass scale was a totally new development that arose out of communist philosophy to alleviate the drudgery of the working woman. Not only was a mass dining room provided in the factory-kitchens, but dinners and semi-cooked food were prepared for the surrounding factories. Equipped with the latest technology, the kitchens could prepare 15,000 meals a day. Like the communal flats, the kitchens never really fulfilled their stated function; at most they were a convenient alternative to eating at home. But the custom of providing semi-cooked meals which could be purchased and taken home from the work place continued throughout the Soviet period.

Housing. As well as cultural buildings, feeding stations and shops, new flats were built for workers to improve their lamentable living conditions. Off this same extended square are some purpose-built apartments of the new type on Traktornaya Street, formerly Krylov Lane, renamed for the first Fordson tractors built under licence at the nearby Krasny Putilov (Kirov) factory. On a narrow plot of land the first new apartments were constructed (1925-27), of fifteen three- and four-storey houses coloured a soft red, designed by Alexander Gegello, Alexander Nikolsky

(1884-1953) and Grigory Simonov (1893-1974), with arches and half-arches connecting the courtyards. Though built of old bricks and other materials from demolished houses as an economy measure, the small houses with their bays, balconies and porches are most successful. Even today, well spaced to provide maximum light and on tree-lined streets and courtyards, they provide attractive accommodation.

School. At the end of Traktornaya on Stachek Prospekt is the local school, one of the first purpose-built after the Revolution. It provided for 1,300 pupils using a modern educational programme. All the classrooms faced south-west or slightly east and thus all had good access to the light. It had all the advantages of a large school — sports hall, laboratories, library, reading room, dining area. The whole building, romantically and somewhat extravagantly, takes the form of a stylised hammer and sickle — the motif which appears over the doorways. When completed with the latest equipment and oak panelling, it was called the 'school-palace' by the local population.

Local Government. Finally, this unique complex was closed off at the southern end by the office building of the Kirov Local Council, the Raisoviet. It was completed in 1934 by Noi Trotsky (no relation), just before the assassination of Sergei Kirov, the Leningrad Party Secretary, probably at Stalin's instigation. After his death Kirov was treated as a hero and many streets, factories, districts, even cities, were named for him. The long, horizontal, four-storey building, with tall tower and square hammer and sickle at one end and round bay at the other, is the epitome of the avant-garde architecture of the time. In front is a wide empty expanse intended for parades and meetings. Later buildings have somewhat obscured the clarity of the scheme and the town council,

128. Interior of the Yelagin Palace by Carlo Rossi (1818-22). The interiors were destroyed by fire at the time of the Revolution, but restored in the 1950s.

129. 'The Doss-house' by
Vladimir Makovsky (1889) in the
Russian Museum depicts a scene
in wintry Moscow of the poor
waiting to enter a doss-house for the night.

130. Paul Gauguin: 'Woman
Holding Fruit', 1893 (Hermitage).

which originally contained offices of both party and local government organisations, is now a sort of civic cum shopping centre.

Moskovsky Prospekt. The idea gradually gained ground of moving the focus of the city from the historic centre south to Moskovsky Prospekt and came to be adopted in the plan of 1935. The theory was that it would be better to build a new socialist Leningrad far away from the old imperial, bourgeois centre; the successful complex of socialist-inspired buildings at the Narva Gate on Stachek Prospekt was one of its inspirations. The sixty-metre-wide road would run south for ten kilometres from the Moscow Triumphal Gate in rather the same relationship as the Narva Gate has to Stachek Prospekt. A large House of Soviets was to be built after an architectural competition and would form the centre of this complex. Noi Trotsky (1895-1940) with others won the competition for the huge structure, 220 metres long and 150 deep. Its construction began in 1936 and was completed just at the outbreak of war in 1941. With its columns, symmetrical wings, sculpture and a frieze, it marks the reintroduction of classical elements in socialist buildings in Leningrad. It is actually only a quarter of its original planned

131. Ilya Repin: 'Bargehaulers on the Volga', 1870-73 (Russian Museum).

size. Since the unpopular plan to move the centre to this part of Leningrad was first interrupted by the war and then finally abandoned, the grandiose size of the building was never justified.

THE WAR

In July 1941 Leningrad began to be surrounded by German forces which completed the encirclement in September. Rationing immediately began, but food supplies were woefully inadequate and after a fire at one of the main warehouses in September, the situation became extremely critical. The daily bread ration fell to only 125 grams. Suffering from constant shelling and the lack of running water and heating, by December over 50,000 citizens a week were dying. The city was just

saved by the ice road over Lake Ladoga, which was the only way to supply the population. The blockade lasted twenty-eight months and it was not finally broken until 27 January 1944, by which time probably over one million people in the city lost their lives.

In 1944, when liberation finally came, the city was a terrible sight, with many buildings in ruins from shells, the weather, and scavenging. It was immediately decided to rebuild the ruins, and by the late fifties Leningrad was whole again, the historic centre once more affirmed. As a matter of pride, even the royal palaces to the west of the city, which had been almost destroyed by the occupying Germans, were rebuilt, restored and refurbished at enormous cost. Piskarev Cemetery, designed by Alexander Vasiliev (b. 1913) and Yevgeny Levinson (1894-1968), where the million who lost their lives in the blockade are buried, conveys at least something of the horror of Leningrad's ordeal by siege. Andrei

132. Kazimir Malevich: 'Red Cavalry', 1926-32 (Russian Museum)

Zhdanov, who was head of the Leningrad Party between 1934 and 1944, after the war directed the campaign against western influence in the arts, particularly hounding the famous Leningrad writers Mikhail Zoshchenko and Anna Akhmatova. The city also suffered architecturally in the Stalin period. It was not spared the ubiquitous tower blocks in the new regions that flank the old centre, but it was fortunate in keeping its centre intact, and so much of the eighteenth- and nineteenth-century

housing stock. Perhaps the fact that it lost the status of capital helped it to keep out of the limelight and retain its architectural integrity in the Soviet period. At the end of the war Nevsky Prospekt, renamed 25th October Prospekt after the Revolution, regained its original name. And in July 1991 in a referendum the population voted by an overwhelming margin to restore the name of St Petersburg. So this historic and beautiful city has come full circle.

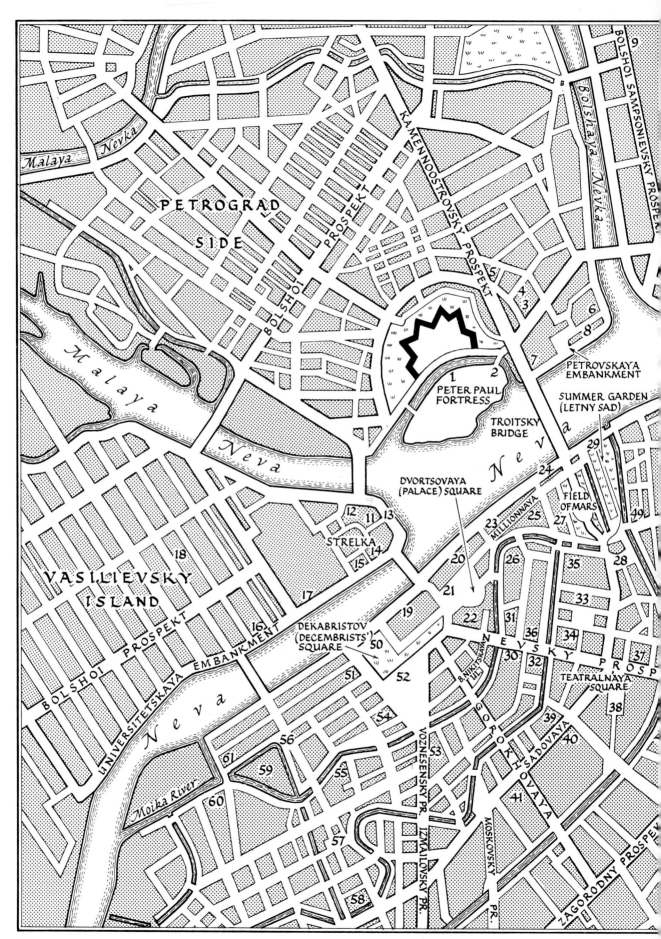

PETROGRAD
SIDE

Malaya Nevka

Bolshoi Sampsonievsky Prospekt

Bolshaya Nevka

Malaya   *Nevka*

Malaya   *Neva*

BOLSHOI PROSPEKT

KAMENNOOSTROVSKY PROSPEKT

9

5

3

6

8

7

PETER PAUL
FORTRESS

1

2

PETROVSKAYA
EMBANKMENT

SUMMER GARDEN
(LETNY SAD)

TROITSKY
BRIDGE

Neva

29

DVORTSOVAYA
(PALACE) SQUARE

24

FIELD
OF MARS

49

MILLIONNAYA

23   25

27

12

11   13

STRELKA

15   14

20   26

35   28

21

33

18

19

22   31   36   34

VASILIEVSKY
ISLAND

DEKABRISTOV
(DECEMBRISTS')
SQUARE

50

30   32

37

17

BOLSHOI PROSPEKT

UNIVERSITETSKAYA EMBANKMENT

16

51   52

NEVSKY PROSP

TEATRALNAYA
SQUARE

GOROKHOVAYA

B. NIKITSKAYA UL.

38

54

39

Neva

56

55

53

40

VOZNESENSKY PR.

IZMAILOVSKY PR.

MOSKOVSKY PR.

SADOVAYA

41

61

59

Moika River

60

57

58

ZAGORODNY PROSPEKT

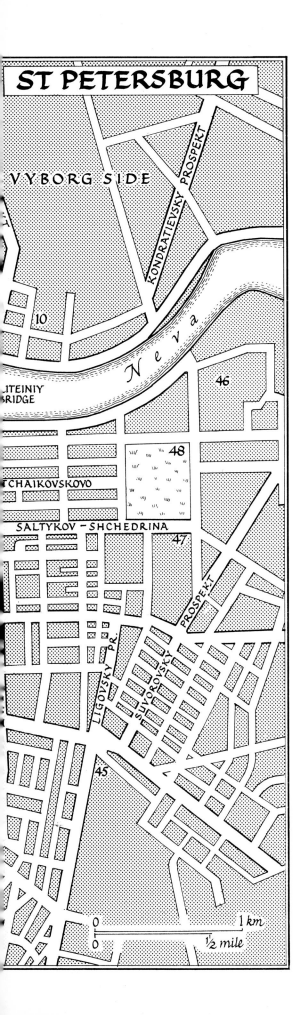

1. Peter Paul Cathedral
2. Peter Gate
3. Kschessinska Mansion
4. Mosque
5. Lidval Building
6. Battleship Aurora
7. Peter the Great Cabin
8. Peter the Great School
9. Sampson Cathedral
10. Finland Station
11. The Exchange
12. Customs House
13. Rostral Column
14. Kunstkamera
15. Academy of Science
16. Academy of Arts
17. Menshikov Palace
18. St Andrew's (Andreevsky) Cathedral
19. Admiralty
20. Winter Palace
21. Alexander Column
22. General Headquarters
23. Grand Duke Vladimir Alexandrovich's Mansion
24. Marble Palace
25. Abamelek-Lazarev House
26. Volkonsky House
27. Pavlovsky Barracks
28. Michael (Engineering) Castle
29. Summer (Letny) Palace
30. Stroganov Palace
31. Guards' Economic Society
32. Kazan Cathedral
33. Michael Palace (Russian Museum)
34. Hotel Europe
35. Church of the Saviour on the Blood
36. Singer Building — House of Books
37. Yeliseyev Emporium
38. Alexander (Pushkin) Theatre
39. State Bank
40. Vorontsov Palace
41. Nikolsky Market
42. Beloselsky-Belozersky Palace
43. Sheremetiev Palace
44. Tolstoi Building
45. Moscow Railway Station
46. Kikin Palata
47. Suvorov Museum
48. Tauride Palace
49. Stieglitz Museum
50. Peter the Great Statue
51. Senate and Synod
52. St Isaac's Cathedral
53. Mariinsky Palace
54. Polovtsov Mansion
55. Yusupov Palace
56. Nicholas Palace
57. Mariinsky (Kirov) Theatre
58. Nicholas Cathedral
59. New Holland Gate
60. Grand Duke Alexis Alexandrovich's Palace
61. Bobrinsky Palace

INDEX

144